Harmful Tax Practices - 2018 Progress Report on Preferential Regimes

INCLUSIVE FRAMEWORK ON BEPS: ACTION 5

This document, as well as any data and any map included herein, are without prejudice to the status of or sovereignty over any territory, to the delimitation of international frontiers and boundaries and to the name of any territory, city or area.

Please cite this publication as:
OECD (2019), *Harmful Tax Practices - 2018 Progress Report on Preferential Regimes: Inclusive Framework on BEPS: Action 5, OECD/G20 Base Erosion and Profit Shifting Project*, OECD Publishing, Paris.
https://doi.org/10.1787/9789264311480-en

ISBN 978-92-64-31147-3 (print)
ISBN 978-92-64-31148-0 (pdf)

Series: OECD/G20 Base Erosion and Profit Shifting Project
ISSN 2313-2604 (print)
ISSN 2313-2612 (online)

Foreword

The integration of national economies and markets has increased substantially in recent years, putting a strain on the international tax rules, which were designed more than a century ago. Weaknesses in the current rules create opportunities for base erosion and profit shifting (BEPS), requiring bold moves by policy makers to restore confidence in the system and ensure that profits are taxed where economic activities take place and value is created.

Following the release of the report Addressing Base Erosion and Profit Shifting in February 2013, OECD and G20 countries adopted a 15-point Action Plan to address BEPS in September 2013. The Action Plan identified 15 actions along three key pillars: introducing coherence in the domestic rules that affect cross-border activities, reinforcing substance requirements in the existing international standards, and improving transparency as well as certainty.

After two years of work, measures in response to the 15 actions were delivered to G20 Leaders in Antalya in November 2015. All the different outputs, including those delivered in an interim form in 2014, were consolidated into a comprehensive package. The BEPS package of measures represents the first substantial renovation of the international tax rules in almost a century. Once the new measures become applicable, it is expected that profits will be reported where the economic activities that generate them are carried out and where value is created. BEPS planning strategies that rely on outdated rules or on poorly co-ordinated domestic measures will be rendered ineffective.

Implementation is now the focus of this work. The BEPS package is designed to be implemented via changes in domestic law and practices, and in tax treaties. With the negotiation of a multilateral instrument (MLI) having been finalised in 2016 to facilitate the implementation of the treaty related BEPS measures, over 80 jurisdictions are covered by the MLI. The entry into force of the MLI on 1 July 2018 paves the way for swift implementation of the treaty related measures. OECD and G20 countries also agreed to continue to work together to ensure a consistent and co-ordinated implementation of the BEPS recommendations and to make the project more inclusive. Globalisation requires that global solutions and a global dialogue be established which go beyond OECD and G20 countries.

A better understanding of how the BEPS recommendations are implemented in practice could reduce misunderstandings and disputes between governments. Greater focus on implementation and tax administration should therefore be mutually beneficial to governments and business. Proposed improvements to data and analysis will help support ongoing evaluation of the quantitative impact of BEPS, as well as evaluating the impact of the countermeasures developed under the BEPS Project.

As a result, the OECD established the Inclusive Framework on BEPS, bringing all interested and committed countries and jurisdictions on an equal footing in the Committee on Fiscal Affairs and all its subsidiary bodies. The Inclusive Framework, which already has more than 120 members, is monitoring and peer reviewing the implementation of the minimum standards as well as completing the work on standard setting to address BEPS issues. In addition to BEPS members, other international organisations and regional tax bodies are involved in the work of the Inclusive Framework, which also consults business and the civil society on its different work streams.

This report was approved by the Inclusive Framework on BEPS on 24 January 2019 and prepared for publication by the OECD Secretariat.

Table of contents

Tables

Figures

Abbreviations and acronyms

BEPS	Base erosion and Profit Shifting
CAN	Consolidated application note
FHTP	Forum on Harmful Tax Practices
IP	Intellectual Property
OECD	Organisation for Economic Co-Operation and Development

Executive summary

1.   BEPS Action 5 is one of the four BEPS minimum standards applicable to all members of the Inclusive Framework on BEPS and any jurisdictions of relevance.[1] At present, 127 jurisdictions have joined the Inclusive Framework and three jurisdictions of relevance have been identified and included in the review process.

2.   Since the start of the BEPS project, the Forum on Harmful Tax Practices ("FHTP") has reviewed a significant number of preferential regimes. The results of these regimes are published in the BEPS Action 5 report (OECD, 2015[1]), the 2017 Progress Report (OECD, 2017[2])and on a regular basis on the OECD's website as new results become available.

3.   Since the publication of the 2017 Progress Report (OECD, 2017[2]) in October 2017, the FHTP has further continued its work on the review of preferential regimes in the scope of BEPS Action 5. In 2017, commitments were made in respect of more than 80 regimes to be made compliant with the BEPS Action 5 minimum standard. In 2018, jurisdictions have in almost all cases delivered on these commitments, with details by jurisdiction contained in Chapter 3 of this Progress Report. In addition, the FHTP has started the review of preferential regimes of new Inclusive Framework members, as well as newly introduced regimes, bringing the total number of regimes reviewed since the start of the BEPS project to 255.

4.   The results to date show that all IP regimes are, with one exception, now either abolished or amended to comply with the nexus approach. These changes mean that it is no longer possible to shift income from IP assets into a preferential regime without having undertaken the underlying research and development activity to create that IP. At the same time, almost all non-IP regimes now contain substantial activities requirements, in order to better ensure the alignment of taxation with the place of value creation.

5.   Where necessary, other changes have been made to comply with the standard. For example, ring-fencing features which were designed to attract investment while protecting the domestic tax base have also been removed by almost all jurisdictions, either by abolishing the regime altogether or opening the regime to the domestic market. In addition, regimes that lacked transparency have also been amended to ensure that the conditions for entry to the regime are clear and known in advance. Finally, all grandfathering provisions will end by 30 June 2021 at the latest.

Figure 1. Results of preferential regime reviews – 255 regimes reviewed as at January 2019

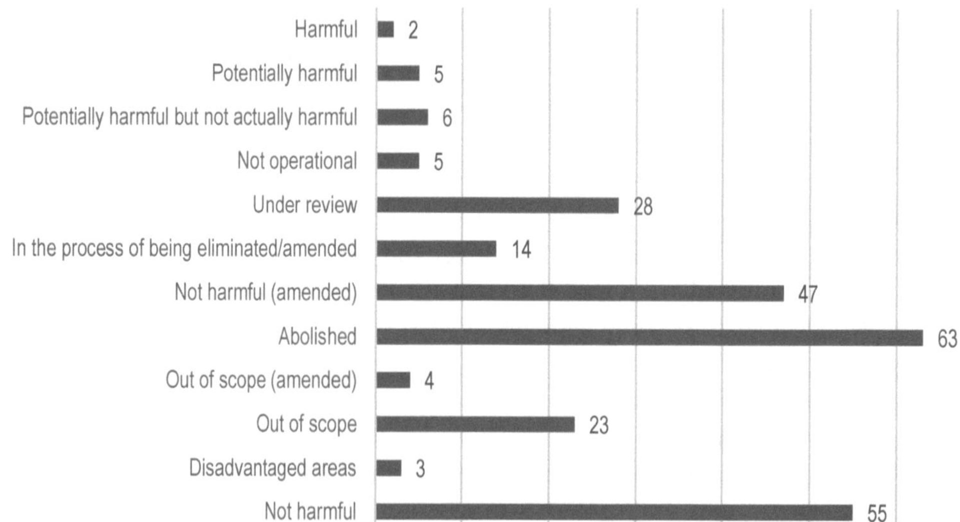

6.   In addition, in 2018 the Inclusive Framework has advanced the work on considering additions or revisions of the framework for harmful tax practices as mandated by the BEPS Action Plan. In this process, the FHTP agreed on a new standard for substantial activities requirements within no or only nominal tax jurisdictions, ensuring a level playing field between those introducing substantial activities requirements in preferential regimes, with those offering a general zero or almost zero corporate tax rate. In addition, in light of the BEPS project and the FHTP's experience in reviewing regimes, it has clarified a number of important issues, including the revision of the key factors and the other factors and providing guidance on the application of these factors for assessing regimes. Annex A of this Progress Report presents the detailed outcomes of this work.[2]

7.   Furthermore, the FHTP has undertaken the second annual review of the transparency framework with results published separately in late 2018 (OECD, 2018[3]).

8.   This Progress Report first sets out the detailed results of the review process by individual regime. It then sets out the next steps to be undertaken by the FHTP in 2019. This includes commencing its work to review the new global standard on substantial activities in no or only nominal tax jurisdictions. The FHTP will continue its work on all relevant issues of harmful tax practices, such as the application of the no or low effective tax rate factor and whether further consideration is needed with respect to territorial tax systems, taking into account the ongoing work within the Inclusive Framework, including on the digital economy. In addition, the FHTP will continue its work to ensure the effectiveness of the standard by expanding the scope of monitoring regarding implementation. One aspect is the grandfathered non-IP regimes, for which details of the relevant data points and process are included in Annex B. Finally, Annex C contains an overview of the work on harmful tax practices that has been published from the 1998 Report (OECD, 1998[4]) until today.

Notes

[1] Some preferential regimes with harmful features may be offered by jurisdictions that are not members of the Inclusive Framework. In order to ensure a level playing field, such jurisdictions are able to be identified by the members of the Inclusive Framework as being relevant to the work and are reviewed according to the same criteria as applies for all other jurisdictions. These are "jurisdictions of relevance".

[2] A part of this work on the resumption of the application of the substantial activity factor to no or only nominal tax jurisdictions, has already been separately published in November 2018 but is incorporated here again for the sake of providing a comprehensive picture of the FHTP's activities.

References

OECD (2018), *Harmful Tax Practices – 2017 Peer Review Reports on the Exchange of Information on Tax Rulings: Inclusive Framework on BEPS: Action 5*, OECD/G20 Base Erosion and Profit Shifting Project, OECD Publishing, Paris, https://dx.doi.org/10.1787/9789264309586-en. [3]

OECD (2017), *Harmful Tax Practices - 2017 Progress Report on Preferential Regimes: Inclusive Framework on BEPS: Action 5*, OECD/G20 Base Erosion and Profit Shifting Project, OECD Publishing, Paris, https://dx.doi.org/10.1787/9789264283954-en. [2]

OECD (2015), *Countering Harmful Tax Practices More Effectively, Taking into Account Transparency and Substance, Action 5 - 2015 Final Report*, OECD/G20 Base Erosion and Profit Shifting Project, OECD Publishing, Paris, https://dx.doi.org/10.1787/9789264241190-en. [1]

OECD (1998), *Harmful Tax Competition: An Emerging Global Issue*, OECD Publishing, Paris, https://dx.doi.org/10.1787/9789264162945-en. [4]

Chapter 1. The FHTP's review of preferential regimes

1.   For more than 20 years, the FHTP has reviewed preferential regimes to ensure that they do not contain features which can negatively impact the tax base of other jurisdictions, and cause a race to the bottom. This process includes a detailed review of applicable legislation and an open dialogue between FHTP members (which, since 2016, comprises all Inclusive Framework members) including the jurisdiction providing the relevant regime. The focus of the work is on preferential regimes that provide benefits to geographically mobile business income (such as income from the provision of intangibles, and financial services), which present a risk of BEPS activity. The review does not include regimes that relate to non-geographically mobile activities such as manufacturing, given that these present an inherently lower risk of BEPS activity. These activities have been out of scope from the FHTP work since the 1998 Report (OECD, 1998[1]).

2.   Inclusive Framework members commit to ensuring that their preferential regimes do not implicate any of the key factors used in the review process, and if they are found to do so, commit to ensure they are amended or abolished. These factors, originally set out in the 1998 Report (OECD, 1998[1])which laid the foundation for the OECD's work on harmful tax practices, have been revised by the Inclusive Framework (as set out in detail in Annex A of this Progress Report) and now consist of five key factors and five other factors.

Table 1.1 Criteria for assessing preferential tax regimes

Five key factors
The regime imposes no or low effective tax rates on income from geographically mobile financial and other service activities.
The regime is ring-fenced from the domestic economy.
The regime lacks transparency.
There is no effective exchange of information with respect to the regime.
The regime fails to require substantial activities.[1]
Five other factors
An artificial definition of the tax base.
Failure to adhere to international transfer pricing principles.
Foreign source income exempt from residence country taxation.
Negotiable tax rate or tax base.
Existence of secrecy provisions.

1. This includes the 2015 Action 5 Final Report (OECD, 2015[2]), the 2017 Progress Report (OECD, 2017[3]), and any guidance on substantial activities agreed by the FHTP and Inclusive Framework thereafter.

3.   Each key factor is briefly described below.

- *The regime imposes no or low effective tax rates on income from geographically mobile financial and other service activities.*

   A low or zero effective tax rate on the relevant income is a necessary starting point for an examination of whether a preferential tax regime is harmful. When a preferential regime benefits income from geographically mobile activities and meets this factor, it is in scope for the FHTP. However, the tax rate factor alone does not imply that a preferential regime is harmful; rather it is a gateway criterion that if met means that the FHTP will continue the review process to determine if one or more of the other key factors are implicated.

- *The regime is ring-fenced from the domestic economy.*

  Some preferential tax regimes are partly or fully insulated from the domestic economy of the jurisdiction providing the regime. The fact that a jurisdiction has designed the regime in a way that protects its own economy from the regime by ring-fencing provides a strong indication that a regime has the potential to create harmful spill-over effects. Ring-fencing focusses on the legal or administrative barriers to participation in the domestic economy, rather than the case where only a small number of domestic taxpayers take advantage of the regime.[1] Ring-fencing may take a number of forms, including:

  - A regime may explicitly or implicitly exclude resident taxpayers from taking advantage of its benefits.
  - Enterprises which benefit from the regime may be explicitly or implicitly prohibited from operating in the domestic market.

- *The regime lacks transparency.*

  A lack of transparency may arise from the way in which a regime is designed and administered. For example, where the details of the regime or its application are not apparent, or there is inadequate regulatory supervision or financial disclosure.

- *There is no effective exchange of information with respect to the regime.*

  When the jurisdiction lacks an effective exchange of information with respect to the regime, this can inhibit the ability of other tax authorities to enforce effectively its rules.

- *The regime encourages operations or arrangements that are purely tax-driven and involve no substantial activities.*

  This factor has been elaborated in the work of the 2015 BEPS Action 5 Report (OECD, 2015), requiring that in order to benefit from a preferential regime, the taxpayer must have engaged in the activities giving rise to the income.

  In the case of regimes that give benefits to income from intellectual property ("IP"), this requirement means being compliant with the "nexus approach" as detailed in the 2015 BEPS Action 5 Report (OECD, 2015[2]). The nexus approach requires a link between the income benefiting from the IP regime and the extent to which the taxpayer has undertaken the underlying research and development that generated the intellectual property. The FHTP uses a substantive approach, reviewing IP regimes that are targeted at IP income (such as patent boxes) as well as regimes that provide for benefits to a wider range of geographically mobile activities but include income from IP (such as certain free zones or international business companies).

  The 2015 BEPS Action 5 Report (OECD, 2015[2]) also contains more general guidance for the application of the substantial activities criterion to non-IP regimes, and further detail on the FHTP's approach is set out in Annex D of the 2017 Progress Report (OECD, 2017[3]). This ensures that the core income generating activities are undertaken, including with an adequate number of full-time, qualified employees and an adequate amount of operating expenditure, supported by a transparent mechanism to ensure compliance.

4.	In many cases, jurisdictions make government commitments to amend or abolish their regimes within a certain time, on the basis of concerns expressed by the FHTP that there are potentially harmful features, and such regimes are found to be "in the process of being amended or eliminated." If the FHTP concludes that a regime meets the no or low effective tax rate factor, and one or more of the other factors applies, it would be found to be potentially harmful, whether in the absence of such a commitment or where such commitment to amend or abolish the regime was not met by the agreed time.

5.	When the FHTP concludes that a regime is potentially harmful, the next step is to assess whether the regime has harmful economic effects. For this assessment, economic data is used (such as number of taxpayers and amount of income benefiting from the regime). When the economic effects shows that the regime is not harmful in practice, the regime is found be potentially harmful but not actually harmful. This means that the jurisdiction does not have to take steps to amend the regime, but the regime is subject to a yearly monitoring process by the FHTP and where changes in economic effects are identified, the conclusion can be revisited. Where a regime is found to be actually harmful, the jurisdiction is expected to amend or abolish the regime in accordance with the FHTP timelines. This includes ensuring that such regimes are quickly closed-off to new applicants and new expansions of business activities, and that any grandfathering is provided for a limited transition period only. These timelines are as follows:

Table 1.2 Timelines for grandfathering

Report	Timelines		
Action 5 Report	The report provides for timelines for IP regimes from OECD/G20 countries, as follows:		
	Cut-off date to benefit from grandfathering	As soon as possible and no later than 30 June 2016 For related party acquired IP assets: 1 January 2016	
	Close-off date (the date the regime is amended / abolished)	As soon as possible and no later than 30 June 2016	
	Grandfathering period (final end date of the regime)	30 June 2021	
2017 Progress Report - Annex B	The report provides for timelines for regimes listed as "in the process of being amended / eliminated" and to which its Annex B applies in the 2017 Progress Report, as follows:[1]		
		IP regimes	Non-IP regimes
	Cut-off date to benefit from grandfathering	As soon as possible and no later than 30 June 2018 For related party acquired IP assets: date of the publication of the Progress Report (16 October 2017)	Date of the publication of the Progress Report (16 October 2017)
	Close-off date (the date the regime is amended/abolished)	As soon as possible and no later than 30 June 2018	One year after the date of the publication of the Progress Report (i.e. 16 October 2018), or where necessary because of the legislative process, by 31 December of the year following the cut-off date (i.e. 31 December 2018)
	Grandfathering period (final end date of the regime)	30 June 2021	30 June 2021

1. New timelines for other IP regimes (e.g. of jurisdictions that joined the Inclusive Framework later) will be published at a later stage.

6.　　　The next chapter presents an update on the status of regimes. The tables include a column for comments that provide additional information as to which potentially harmful aspects have been removed, if grandfathering has been provided, if the regime was newly introduced by the jurisdiction and any other relevant details.

Notes

[1] See Annex A – paragraph 77 for further discussion.

References

OECD (2017), *Harmful Tax Practices - 2017 Progress Report on Preferential Regimes: Inclusive Framework on BEPS: Action 5*, OECD/G20 Base Erosion and Profit Shifting Project, OECD Publishing, Paris, https://dx.doi.org/10.1787/9789264283954-en.　[3]

OECD (2015), *Countering Harmful Tax Practices More Effectively, Taking into Account Transparency and Substance, Action 5 - 2015 Final Report*, OECD/G20 Base Erosion and Profit Shifting Project, OECD Publishing, Paris, https://dx.doi.org/10.1787/9789264241190-en.　[2]

OECD (1998), *Harmful Tax Competition: An Emerging Global Issue*, OECD Publishing, Paris, https://dx.doi.org/10.1787/9789264162945-en.　[1]

Chapter 2. Update on the status of regimes

14.   This part provides an update on the status of preferential tax regimes that have been reviewed by the FHTP. In all of the following tables, the meaning of the relevant terms is as follows:

Table 2.1. Meaning of results for preferential tax regimes

Result	Meaning
Harmful	The regime has harmful features and economic effects. The jurisdiction is expected to take measures in order to remove the harmful features of the regime.
Potentially harmful but not actually harmful	The regime is in scope, meets the low or no effective tax rate criterion and implicates one or more of the criteria, but an assessment of the economic effects shows that the regime is not having a harmful impact in practice. The regime is subject to a yearly monitoring process by the FHTP and where changes are identified, the FHTP can reconsider the conclusion.
Potentially harmful	The regime is in scope, meets the low or no effective tax rate criterion and features of the regime implicate one or more of the criteria. However, an assessment of the economic effects has not yet taken place to make a determination as to whether the regime is (actually) "harmful".
Not harmful	The regime is in scope but does not have any features which implicate any of the criteria.
Not harmful (amended)	The regime is not harmful, taking into account amendments to ensure harmful features are removed.
Out of scope	The regime does not grant tax benefits to geographically mobile activities.
Out of scope (amended)	The regime is out of scope, taking in account amendments which means it no longer grants tax benefits to geographically mobile activities.
In the process of being amended / in the process of being eliminated	The jurisdiction has communicated to the FHTP the commitment of its government to abolish or amend the regime in light of the discussions by the FHTP about the features of the regime that are of concern, For regimes reviewed in 2017 and thereafter, this commitment involves a commitment to making the amendments within the timeline indicated above.
Abolished	A definite date for complete abolition of the regime has been announced, and the regime is transparent and has effective exchange of information. No new entrants are permitted into the regime. Any grandfathering for existing beneficiaries is consistent with the applicable framework and timelines.
Disadvantaged areas regime	The regime provides incidental benefits to IP income, which is acceptable under paragraph 150 of the 2015 BEPS Action 5 Report (OECD, 2015[1]).
Not operational	The jurisdiction did not operationalise the regime and no taxpayer is able to benefit from it. If the regime becomes operational in the future, the jurisdiction has committed to inform the FHTP and the regime will be reviewed.
Under review	The FHTP is continuing to consider the features of the regime and whether the criteria are implicated.

Regimes listed in the 2015 BEPS Action 5 report

15.   These tables present an update on the status of regimes listed in the 2015 BEPS Action 5 Report (OECD, 2015[1]).

Table 2.2. IP regimes

	Jurisdiction	Regime	Status	Comments
1.	Belgium	Deduction for innovation income	Not harmful (amended)	Substance requirements (nexus approach) in place. Grandfathering in accordance with FHTP timelines.
2.	China (People's Republic of)	Reduced rate for high & new tech enterprises	Not harmful[1]	No harmful features.
3.	Colombia	Software regime	Abolished	No grandfathering provided.
4.	France	Reduced corporation tax rate on IP income[2]	Not harmful (amended)	Substance requirements (nexus approach) in place. No grandfathering provided.
5.	Hungary	IP regime for royalties and capital gains	Not harmful (amended)	Substance requirements (nexus approach) in place. Grandfathering in accordance with FHTP timelines.
6.	Israel	Amended preferred enterprise regime	Not harmful (amended)	Substance requirements (nexus approach) in place. Grandfathering in accordance with FHTP timelines.
7.	Italy	Taxation of income from intangible assets	Not harmful (amended) except for the extension to new entrants for trademark[3] between 1 July 2016 and 31 December 2016, which is harmful	Substance requirements (nexus approach) in place and grandfathering in accordance with FHTP timelines, except for extension as noted.
8.	Luxembourg	Partial exemption for income/gains derived from certain IP rights	Abolished	Grandfathering in accordance with FHTP timelines.
9.	Netherlands	Innovation box	Not harmful (amended)	Substance requirements (nexus approach) in place. Grandfathering in accordance with FHTP timelines.
10.	Portugal	Partial exemption for income from certain intangible property	Not harmful (amended)	Substance requirements (nexus approach) in place. Grandfathering in accordance with FHTP timelines.
11.	Spain	Partial exemption for income from certain intangible assets (Federal regime)	Not harmful (amended)[4]	Substance requirements (nexus approach) in place. Grandfathering in accordance with FHTP timelines.
12.	Spain	Partial exemption for income from certain intangible assets (Basque country)	Not harmful (amended)[5]	Substance requirements (nexus approach) in place. Grandfathering in accordance with FHTP timelines.
13.	Spain	Partial exemption for income from certain intangible assets (Navarra)	Not harmful (amended)[6]	Substance requirements (nexus approach) in place. Grandfathering in accordance with FHTP timelines.
14.	Switzerland - Canton of Nidwalden	Licence box	Not harmful (amended)	Substance requirements (nexus approach) in place. Grandfathering in accordance with FHTP timelines.

	Jurisdiction	Regime	Status	Comments
15.	Turkey	Technology development zones regime	Not harmful (amended) except for the extension to new entrants between 1 July 2016 and 19 October 2017, which is harmful	Substance requirements (nexus approach) in place and grandfathering in accordance with FHTP timelines, except for extension as noted.
16.	United Kingdom	Patent box	Not harmful (amended)	Substance requirements (nexus approach) in place. Grandfathering in accordance with FHTP timelines.

Note: See table 6.1 of the 2015 BEPS Action 5 Report (OECD, 2015[1]).

1. While the regime did not technically comply with the nexus approach, it was considered functionally equivalent and therefore evaluated as not harmful, given its distinct features and safeguards and the willingness of China to provide additional information.

2. Formerly known as "Reduced rate for long term capital gains and profits from the licensing of IP rights".

3. The Italian IP regime did not and does not include in the eligible assets any marketing related assets other than trademarks.

4. Spain's partial exemption for income from certain intangible assets was inconsistent with the nexus approach for IP assets acquired from related parties for the period from 1 January 2017 to 31 December 2017 and for new taxpayers entering the regime in the period from 1 July 2016 to 31 December 2017.

5. See previous table note.

6. See previous table note.

Table 2.3. Non-IP regimes

	Jurisdiction	Regime	Status	Comments
1.	Argentina	Promotional regime for software industry	Not harmful	No harmful features.
2.	Australia	Conduit foreign income	Not harmful	No harmful features.
3.	Brazil	PADIS – Semiconductors industry	Not harmful	No harmful features.
4.	Canada	Life insurance business	Potentially harmful but not actually harmful	Ring-fencing implicated, but no harmful economic effects in practice. Regime is subject to annual monitoring.
5.	China (People's Republic of)	Reduced rate for advanced technology services enterprises	Not harmful	No harmful features.
6.	Colombia	Foreign portfolio investment	Not harmful[1]	No harmful features.
7.	Greece	Offshore engineering and construction	Not harmful (amended)	Ring-fencing removed. No grandfathering provided
8.	India	Deductions in respect of certain incomes of offshore banking units and international financial services centre	Not harmful	No harmful features.
9.	India	Special provisions in respect of newly established units in special economic zones	Not harmful	No harmful features.
10.	India	Special provisions relating to income of shipping companies – tonnage tax scheme	Not harmful	No harmful features.
11.	India	Taxation of profit and gains of life insurance business	Not harmful	No harmful features.
12.	Indonesia	Public / listed company regime	Out of scope	No income from geographically mobile activities.
13.	Indonesia	Investment allowance regime	Out of scope	No income from geographically mobile activities.

	Jurisdiction	Regime	Status	Comments
14.	Indonesia	Special economic zone regime	Out of scope	No income from geographically mobile activities.
15.	Indonesia	Tax holiday regime	Out of scope	No income from geographically mobile activities.
16.	Japan	Special zones for international competitiveness development	Not harmful[2]	No harmful features.
17.	Japan	Measures for the promotion of research and development	Not harmful[3]	No harmful features.
18.	Latvia	Shipping taxation regime	Not harmful	No harmful features.
19.	Latvia	Special economic zones	Disadvantaged areas regime	Subject to monitoring to ensure continued low risk of BEPS.
20.	Luxembourg	Private asset management company (Société de gestion de patrimoine familial)	Not harmful[4]	No harmful features.
21.	Luxembourg	Investment company in risk capital (Société d'investissement en capital à risque)	Not harmful[5]	No harmful features.
22.	South Africa	Headquarter company	Potentially harmful but not actually harmful	Ring-fencing implicated, but no harmful economic effects in practice. Regime is subject to annual monitoring.
23.	South Africa	Exemption of income in respect of ships used in international shipping	Not harmful	No harmful features.
24.	Switzerland – cantonal level	Auxiliary company regime (previously referred to as domiciliary company regime)	In the process of being eliminated[6]	Regular reporting on progress is provided to FHTP.
25.	Switzerland – cantonal level	Mixed company regime	In the process of being eliminated[7]	Regular reporting on progress is provided to FHTP.
26.	Switzerland – cantonal level	Holding company regime	In the process of being eliminated[8]	Regular reporting on progress is provided to FHTP.
27.	Switzerland – federal level	Commissionaire ruling regime	In the process of being eliminated[9]	Regular reporting on progress is provided to FHTP.
28.	Switzerland – federal level	Newly established or re-designed enterprises	Disadvantaged areas regime	Subject to monitoring to ensure continued low risk of BEPS.
29.	Turkey	Shipping regime	Not harmful	No harmful features.

Note: See table 6.2 of the 2015 BEPS Action 5 Report (OECD, 2015[1]).
1. This conclusion was reached by the FHTP without reaching any conclusion that Colombia's regime was within the scope of the work of the FHTP.
2. This regime was considered prior to the approval of the BEPS Action Plan.
3. See previous table note.
4. See previous table note.
5. See previous table note.
6. The tax reform bill, approved in June 2016 by the Federal Parliament was rejected by the Swiss voters on 12 February 2017. The Swiss Government immediately initiated steps for a new proposal to abolish the regimes. The new federal legislation was approved by Parliament on 28 September 2018. Subject to the Swiss constitutional approval process, the intention is for the reform to become effective by 1 January 2020.
7. See previous table note.
8. See previous table note.
9. See previous table note.

Regimes not listed in the 2015 BEPS Action 5 report

16.   The following tables present the results of the review of preferential regimes that are not listed in the 2015 BEPS Action 5 report (OECD, 2015[1]) and that have been reviewed since October 2015, as at 24 January 2019. The results are presented according to the categories of regime.

Table 2.4. IP regimes

	Jurisdiction	Regime	Status	Comments
1.	Andorra	Special regime for exploitation of certain intangibles[1]	Not harmful (amended)	Substance requirements (nexus approach) in place. Grandfathering in accordance with FHTP timelines.
2.	Curaçao	Innovation box	Not harmful	New regime, designed in compliance with FHTP standards.
3.	Greece	Tax patent incentives	Under review	Regime under review by FHTP.
4.	India	Tax on income from patent	Not harmful	Substance requirements (nexus approach) in place
5.	Ireland	Knowledge development box	Not harmful	New regime, designed in compliance with FHTP standards.
6.	Israel	Preferred technological enterprise regime	Not harmful	New regime, designed in compliance with FHTP standards.
7.	Korea	Special taxation for transfer, acquisition, etc. of technology	Not harmful (amended)	Substance requirements (nexus approach) in place. No grandfathering provided.
8.	Liechtenstein	IP box	Abolished	Grandfathering in accordance with FHTP timelines.
9.	Lithuania	IP regime	Not harmful	New regime, designed in compliance with FHTP standards.
10.	Luxembourg	IP regime	Not harmful	New regime, designed in compliance with FHTP standards.
11.	Malta	Patent box	Abolished	Grandfathering in accordance with FHTP timelines.
12.	Panama	City of knowledge technical zone	Not harmful (amended)	Substance requirements (nexus approach) in place. No grandfathering provided.
13.	Panama	General IP regime	Not harmful	New regime, designed in compliance with FHTP standards.
14.	San Marino	IP regime provided by law no. 102/2004	Abolished	No grandfathering provided.
15.	San Marino	IP regime	Not harmful	New regime, designed in compliance with FHTP standards.
16.	Singapore	IP development incentive	Not harmful[2]	New regime, designed in compliance with FHTP standards.
17.	Slovak Republic	Patent-box	Not harmful	New regime, designed in compliance with FHTP standards.
18.	Turkey	5/B regime	Not harmful	New regime, designed in compliance with FHTP standards.
19.	Viet Nam	IP benefits	Under review	Regime under review by FHTP.
IP regimes that are also reviewed as non-IP regimes[3]				
20.	Aruba	Exempt company	In the process of being eliminated/amended	Potentially harmful features will be addressed.

	Jurisdiction	Regime	Status	Comments
21.	Barbados	International business companies	Abolished	Grandfathering in accordance with FHTP timelines.
22.	Barbados	International societies with restricted liability	Abolished	Grandfathering in accordance with FHTP timelines.
23.	Belize	International business companies	Abolished	Grandfathering in accordance with FHTP timelines.
24.	Botswana	International financial services company	Abolished	No grandfathering provided.
25.	Brunei Darussalam	Pioneer services companies	Under review	Regime under review by FHTP.
26.	Curaçao	Curaçao investment company[4]	Not harmful (amended)	Substance requirements (nexus approach) in place. No grandfathering provided.
27.	Curaçao	Export facility	Abolished	No grandfathering provided.
28.	Jordan	Aqaba special economic zone	Under review	Regime under review by FHTP.
29.	Jordan	Development zone	Potentially harmful	Ring-fencing addressed; substance requirements (nexus approach) not yet addressed.
30.	Kazakhstan	Special economic zones	Under review	Regime under review by FHTP.
31.	Kenya	Special economic zone	Not operational	Regime not operational.
32.	Lithuania	Free economic zone taxation regime	Disadvantaged areas regime	Subject to monitoring to ensure continued low risk of BEPS.
33.	Macau (China)	Macau offshore institution	Abolished	Grandfathering in accordance with FHTP timelines.
34.	Malaysia	Biotechnology industry	Abolished	Grandfathering in accordance with FHTP timelines.
35.	Malaysia	MSC Malaysia	Abolished	Grandfathering in accordance with FHTP timelines.
36.	Malaysia	Pioneer status – High technology	Out of scope (amended)	No income from geographically mobile activities. Grandfathering in accordance with FHTP timelines.
37.	Malaysia	Principal hub	Abolished	Grandfathering in accordance with FHTP timelines.
38.	Mauritius	Global business license 1	Abolished	Grandfathering in accordance with FHTP timelines.
39.	Mauritius	Global business license 2	Abolished	Grandfathering in accordance with FHTP timelines.
40.	Mongolia	Free trade zones	In the process of being eliminated	Potentially harmful features will be addressed.
41.	Paraguay	Investment of capital from abroad	Under review	Regime under review by FHTP.
42.	Saint Kitts and Nevis	Companies act	Under review	Regime under review by FHTP.
43.	Saint Kitts and Nevis	Nevis business corporation	Under review	Regime under review by FHTP.
44.	Saint Kitts and Nevis	Nevis LLC	Under review	Regime under review by FHTP.
45.	Saint Lucia	International business company	Abolished[5]	Grandfathering in accordance with FHTP timelines.
46.	Saint Lucia	International partnership	Abolished[6]	Grandfathering in accordance with FHTP timelines.
47.	Saint Lucia	International trust	Abolished[7]	Grandfathering in accordance with FHTP timelines.

	Jurisdiction	Regime	Status	Comments
48.	Saint Vincent and the Grenadines	International business companies	Abolished	Grandfathering in accordance with FHTP timelines.
49.	Saint Vincent and the Grenadines	International trusts	Abolished	Grandfathering in accordance with FHTP timelines.
50.	San Marino	New companies regime provided by art. 73, law no. 166/2013	Not harmful (amended)	Substance requirements (nexus approach) in place. Grandfathering in accordance with FHTP timelines.
51.	San Marino	Regime for high-tech start-up companies under law no. 71/2013 and delegated decree no. 116/2014	Not harmful (amended)	Substance requirements (nexus approach) in place. Grandfathering in accordance with FHTP timelines.
52.	Seychelles	Companies special license	Abolished	Grandfathering in accordance with FHTP timelines.
53.	Seychelles	International business companies	Abolished	No grandfathering provided.
54.	Seychelles	International trade zone	Abolished	Grandfathering in accordance with FHTP timelines.
55.	Singapore	Development and expansion incentive - services	Abolished	Grandfathering in accordance with FHTP timelines.
56.	Singapore	Pioneer service company	Abolished	Grandfathering in accordance with FHTP timelines.
57.	Thailand	International headquarters and treasury centre	Not operational	No grandfathering provided.
58.	Thailand	Regional operating headquarters 1	Not operational	No grandfathering provided.
59.	Thailand	Regional operating headquarters 2	Not operational	No grandfathering provided.
60.	United States	Foreign-derived intangible income (FDII)	Under review	Regime under review by FHTP.
61.	Uruguay	Benefits under law 16.906 for biotechnology	Abolished	No grandfathering provided.
62.	Uruguay	Benefits under lit S art. 52 for biotechnology and for software	Not harmful (amended)	Substance requirements (nexus approach) in place. Grandfathering in accordance with FHTP timelines.
63.	Uruguay	Free zones	Not harmful (amended)	Substance requirements (nexus approach) in place. No grandfathering provided.
64.	Viet Nam	Export processing zone	Out of scope	No income from geographically mobile activities.

1. Formerly known as "Companies involved in the international exploitation of intangible assets".
2. Subject to final adoption of new legislation.
3. Some preferential regimes provides for benefits to both income from IP and other non-IP geographically mobile activities. These "dual category" regimes are reviewed as both an IP regime and a non-IP regime and therefore have to comply with both substantial activities requirements and two separate conclusions are applicable to the regime.
4. Formerly known as "Tax exempt entity".
5. Subject to final adoption of new legislation closing the grandfathered regime to IP assets acquired from related parties.
6. Subject to final adoption of new legislation closing the grandfathered regime to IP assets acquired from related parties.
7. Subject to final adoption of new legislation closing the grandfathered regime to IP assets acquired from related parties.

Table 2.5. Headquarters regimes

	Jurisdiction	Regime	Status	Comments
1.	Barbados	International business companies[1]	Abolished[2]	Grandfathering provided, see table note.
2.	Chile	Business platform regime	Potentially harmful but not actually harmful From 1 January 2022: Abolished[3]	Ring-fencing factor implicated, but no harmful economic effects in practice. Regime is subject to annual monitoring.
3.	Kenya	Special economic zone[4]	Not operational	Regime not operational.
4.	Malaysia	Principal hub[5]	In the process of being amended	Substantial activities factor addressed; ring-fencing not yet addressed.
5.	Mauritius	Global business license 1	Abolished	Grandfathering in accordance with FHTP timelines.
6.	Mauritius	Global business license 2	Abolished	Grandfathering in accordance with FHTP timelines.
7.	Mauritius	Global headquarters administration regime	Not harmful	No harmful features.
8.	Panama	Multinational headquarters	Not harmful (amended)	Ring-fencing removed. Substance requirements (non-IP) in place. Grandfathering in accordance with FHTP timelines.
9.	Philippines	Regional or area headquarters	Out of scope	No income from geographically mobile activities.
10.	Philippines	Regional operating headquarters	In the process of being eliminated	Potentially harmful features will be addressed
11.	Seychelles	Companies special license[6]	Abolished	Grandfathering in accordance with FHTP timelines.
12.	Singapore	Development and expansion incentive – services	Not harmful	No harmful features.
13.	Singapore	Pioneer service company	Not harmful	No harmful features.
14.	Thailand	International headquarters and treasury centre	Potentially harmful[7]	Grandfathering beyond FHTP timelines.
15.	Thailand	Regional operating headquarters 1	Abolished[8]	Grandfathering provided, see table note.
16.	Thailand	Regional operating headquarters 2	Potentially harmful[9]	Grandfathering beyond FHTP timelines.
17.	Turkey	Regional headquarters / regional management centre	Out of scope	No income from geographically mobile activities.

1. Also reviewed as a financing and leasing regime.
2. Subject to the confirmation of the closure of the grandfathered regime to new activities and new assets, which will be verified by the FHTP at the next opportunity.
3. In accordance with Law No. 21,047 no new taxpayers will benefit from this regime as from 23 November 2017. With regard to existing business platform companies, the law provides for a grandfathering period which expires by 31 December 2021. Therefore, this regime will be considered completely abolished by 1 January 2022.
4. Also reviewed as a distribution and service centre regime.
5. Also reviewed as a financing and leasing regime.
6. Also reviewed as a financing and leasing regime.
7. The regime has been abolished, however due to legal constraints the benefits of the regime remain available after 30 June 2021, beyond the agreed FHTP timelines.
8. Subject to the confirmation of the closure of the grandfathered regime to new activities, which will be verified by the FHTP at the next opportunity.
9. The regime has been abolished, however due to legal constraints the benefits of the regime remain available after 30 June 2021, beyond the agreed FHTP timelines.

Table 2.6. Financing and leasing regimes

	Jurisdiction	Regime	Status	Comments
1.	Antigua and Barbuda	International business corporations	Abolished	No grandfathering provided.
2.	Andorra	Intercompany and financing regime	Abolished	Grandfathering in accordance with FHTP timelines.
3.	Aruba	Exempt company	In the process of being eliminated/amended	Potentially harmful features will be addressed.
4.	Barbados	International business companies[1]	Abolished[2]	Grandfathering provided, see table note.
5.	Barbados	International financial services	Abolished[3]	Grandfathering provided, see table note.
6.	Barbados	International trusts[4]	Abolished	No grandfathering provided.
7.	Belize	International business companies	Not harmful (amended)	Ring-fencing removed. Substance requirements (non-IP) in place. Grandfathering in accordance with FHTP timelines.
8.	Botswana	International financial services company	Not harmful (amended)	Ring-fencing removed. No grandfathering provided.
9.	Curaçao	Curaçao investment company[5]	Not harmful (amended)	Substance requirements (non-IP) in place. No grandfathering provided.
10.	Georgia	International financial company	Potentially harmful but not actually harmful	Ring-fencing implicated, but no harmful economic effects in practice. Regime is subject to annual monitoring.
11.	Hong Kong (China)	Profits tax concession for corporate treasury centres	Not harmful (amended)	Ring-fencing removed. No grandfathering provided.
12.	Hong Kong (China)	Profits tax concessions for aircraft lessors and aircraft leasing managers	Not harmful	No harmful features.
13.	Kazakhstan	AIFC	Under review	Regime under review by FHTP.
14.	Malaysia	Treasury management centre	Abolished	Grandfathering in accordance with FHTP timelines.
15.	Malaysia	Labuan leasing	Not harmful (amended)	Ring-fencing removed. Substance requirements (non-IP) in place. No grandfathering provided.
16.	Malaysia	Principal hub[6]	In the process of being amended	Substantial activities factor addressed; ring-fencing not yet addressed.
17.	Mauritius	Global treasury activities	Not harmful	No harmful features.
18.	Montserrat	International business companies	Potentially harmful but not actually harmful	Ring-fencing implicated, but no harmful economic effects in practice. Regime is subject to annual monitoring.
19.	Saint Kitts and Nevis	Nevis LLC	Under review	Regime under review by FHTP.
20.	Saint Kitts and Nevis	Nevis business corporation	Under review	Regime under review by FHTP.
21.	Saint Kitts and Nevis	Companies act	Under review	Regime under review by FHTP.
22.	Saint Lucia	International business company	Abolished[7]	Grandfathering in accordance with FHTP timelines.

	Jurisdiction	Regime	Status	Comments
23.	Saint Lucia	International trusts[8]	Abolished	Grandfathering in accordance with FHTP timelines.
24.	Saint Lucia	International partnership	Abolished[9]	Grandfathering in accordance with FHTP timelines.
25.	Saint Vincent and the Grenadines	International business companies	Abolished	Grandfathering in accordance with FHTP timelines.
26.	Saint Vincent and the Grenadines	International trusts[10]	Abolished	Grandfathering in accordance with FHTP timelines.
27.	San Marino	Financing regime provided by law no. 102/2004	Abolished	No grandfathering provided.
28.	Seychelles	International business companies	Abolished	No grandfathering provided.
29.	Seychelles	Companies special license[11]	Abolished	Grandfathering in accordance with FHTP timelines.
30.	Singapore	Aircraft leasing scheme	Not harmful	No harmful features.
31.	Singapore	Finance and treasury centre	Not harmful	No harmful features.
32.	Sint Maarten	Tax exempt company	Under review	Regime under review by FHTP. Jurisdiction affected by hurricane.

1. Also reviewed as a headquarters regime.
2. Subject to the confirmation of the closure of the grandfathered regime to new activities and new assets, which will be verified by the FHTP at the next opportunity.
3. Subject to the confirmation of the closure of the grandfathered regime to new activities, which will be verified by the FHTP at the next opportunity.
4. Also reviewed as a holding company regime.
5. Formerly known as "Tax exempt entity".
6. Also reviewed as a headquarters regime.
7. Subject to final adoption of new legislation closing the grandfathered regime to new activities and new assets.
8. Also reviewed as a holding company regime.
9. Subject to final adoption of new legislation closing the grandfathered regime to new activities and new assets
10. Also reviewed as a holding company regime.
11. Also reviewed as a headquarters regime.

Table 2.7. Banking and insurance regimes

	Jurisdiction	Regime	Status	Comments
1.	Antigua and Barbuda	International banking	Abolished	No grandfathering provided.
2.	Australia	Offshore banking unit	In the process of being amended	Potentially harmful features will be addressed.
3.	Barbados	Exempt insurance	Abolished[1]	Grandfathering provided, see table note.
4.	Barbados	Qualifying insurance companies	Abolished	Grandfathering in accordance with FHTP timelines.
5.	Barbados	Insurance regime	Not harmful	New regime, designed in compliance with FHTP standards.
6.	Canada	International banking centres	Abolished	No grandfathering provided.
7.	Hong Kong (China)	Profits tax concession for professional reinsurers	Not harmful (amended)	Ring-fencing removed. No grandfathering provided.
8.	Hong Kong (China)	Profits tax concession for captive insurers	Not harmful (amended)	Ring-fencing removed. No grandfathering provided.
9.	Macau (China)	Macau offshore institution	Abolished	Grandfathering in accordance with FHTP timelines.

	Jurisdiction	Regime	Status	Comments
10.	Malaysia	Re-insurance and re-takaful business[2]	Not harmful (amended)	Grandfathering in accordance with FHTP timelines.
11.	Malaysia	Labuan financial services	Not harmful (amended)	Ring-fencing removed. Substance requirements (non-IP) in place. Grandfathering in accordance with FHTP timelines.
12.	Mauritius	Captive insurance	Not harmful (amended)	Substance requirements (non-IP) in place. Grandfathering in accordance with FHTP timelines.
13.	Mauritius	Banks holding a banking licence under the Banking Act 2004 ('Segment B banking')	Abolished	Grandfathering in accordance with FHTP timelines.
14.	Mauritius	Banks holding a banking licence under the Banking Act 2004	Not harmful	New regime, designed in compliance with FHTP standards.
15.	Mauritius	Investment banking	Not harmful	No harmful features.
16.	Nigeria	Free trade zones[3]	Under review	Regime under review by FHTP.
17.	Seychelles	Non-domestic insurance business	Abolished	Grandfathering in accordance with FHTP timelines.
18.	Seychelles	Offshore banking	Abolished	No grandfathering provided.
19.	Seychelles	Fund administration business	Not harmful (amended)	Substance requirements (non-IP) in place. Grandfathering in accordance with FHTP timelines.
20.	Seychelles	Securities businesses under the securities act	Not harmful (amended)	Substance requirements (non-IP) in place. Grandfathering in accordance with FHTP timelines.
21.	Seychelles	Reinsurance business	Abolished	No grandfathering provided.
22.	Singapore	Insurance business development	Not harmful (amended)	Ring-fencing removed. Grandfathering in accordance with FHTP timelines.
23.	Singapore	Financial sector incentive	Not harmful	No harmful features.
24.	Thailand	International banking facilities	Abolished	Grandfathering in accordance with FHTP timelines.

1. Subject to the confirmation of the closure of the grandfathered regime to new activities, which will be verified by the FHTP at the next opportunity.
2. Formerly known as "Inward re-insurance and offshore insurance".
3. Also reviewed as a distribution and service centre regime.

Table 2.8. Distribution centre and service centre regimes

	Jurisdiction	Regime	Status	Comments
1.	Andorra	Companies involved in international trade	Abolished	Grandfathering in accordance with FHTP timelines.
2.	Aruba	Free zone	In the process of being eliminated/amended	Potentially harmful features will be addressed.
3.	Barbados	Fiscal incentives act	Out of scope	No income from geographically mobile activities.

	Jurisdiction	Regime	Status	Comments
4.	Costa Rica	Free trade zone	Not harmful (amended)[1]	Ring-fencing removed. Substance requirements (non-IP) in place. No grandfathering provided.
5.	Curaçao	Export facility	Abolished	No grandfathering provided.
6.	Curaçao	E-Zone	Out of scope (amended)	Income from geographically mobile activities removed. No grandfathering provided.
7.	Gabon	Special economic zone	Under review	Regime under review by FHTP.
8.	Georgia	Free industrial zone	Out of scope	No income from geographically mobile activities.
9.	Georgia	Special trade company	Out of scope	No income from geographically mobile activities.
10.	Georgia	Virtual zone person	Potentially harmful but not actually harmful	Ring-fencing and substantial activities factor implicated, but no harmful economic effects in practice. Regime is subject to annual monitoring.
11.	Jordan	Aqaba special economic zone	Under review	Regime under review by FHTP.
12.	Jordan	Development zones	Potentially harmful	Ring-fencing addressed; substance requirements (non-IP) not yet addressed.
13.	Jordan	Free trade zones	Abolished	No grandfathering provided.
14.	Kazakhstan	Special economic zones	Under review	Regime under review by FHTP.
15.	Kenya	Export processing zone	Out of scope	No income from geographically mobile activities.
16.	Kenya	Special economic zone[2]	Not operational	Regime not operational.
17.	Korea	Foreign investment zone	Out of scope	No income from geographically mobile activities.
18.	Korea	Free economic zone / free trade zone	Out of scope	No income from geographically mobile activities.
19.	Lithuania	Free economic zone taxation regime	Not harmful	No harmful features.
20.	Malaysia	Approved service projects	Out of scope	No income from geographically mobile activities.
21.	Malaysia	Green technology services	Not harmful	No harmful features.
22.	Malaysia	Malaysian international trading company	Out of scope	No income from geographically mobile activities.
23.	Malaysia	Special economic regions	Not harmful (amended)	Ring-fencing removed. Substance requirements (non-IP) in place. Grandfathering in accordance with FHTP timelines.
24.	Mauritius	Freeport zone	Out of scope (amended)	Income from geographically mobile activities removed. Grandfathering in accordance with FHTP timelines.
25.	Mongolia	Free trade zones	In the process of being eliminated	Potentially harmful features will be addressed.
26.	Nigeria	Free trade zones[3]	Under review	Regime under review by FHTP.
27.	Panama	Colon free zone	Out of scope	No income from geographically mobile activities.

	Jurisdiction	Regime	Status	Comments
28.	Panama	Panama-Pacifico special economic zone	Not harmful (amended)	Ring-fencing removed. Substance requirements (non-IP) in place. Grandfathering in accordance with FHTP timelines.
29.	Paraguay	Free zone	Out of scope	No income from geographically mobile activities.
30.	Peru	Special economic zone 1 (Ceticos / ZED)	Out of scope	No income from geographically mobile activities.
31.	Peru	Special economic zone 2 (Zofratacna)	Not harmful	No harmful features.
32.	Saint Kitts and Nevis	Fiscal incentives act	Out of scope	No income from geographically mobile activities.
33.	Seychelles	International trade zone	Out of scope (amended)	No income from geographically mobile activities. Grandfathering in accordance with FHTP timelines
34.	Singapore	Global trader programme	Not harmful	No harmful features.
35.	Thailand	International trade centre	Potentially harmful[4]	Grandfathering beyond FHTP timelines.
36.	Trinidad and Tobago	Free trade zones	In the process of being eliminated[5]	Potentially harmful features will be addressed.
37.	Uruguay	Free zones	Not harmful (amended)	Ring-fencing removed. Substance requirements (non-IP) in place. Grandfathering in accordance with FHTP timelines.
38.	Uruguay	Shared service centre	Not harmful (amended)	Ring-fencing removed. No grandfathering provided.
39.	Viet Nam	Disadvantaged areas	Under review	Regime under review by FHTP.
40.	Viet Nam	Economic zones	Under review	Regime under review by FHTP.
41.	Viet Nam	Export processing zone	Out of scope	No income from geographically mobile activities.
42.	Viet Nam	Industrial parks/zones	Out of scope	No income from geographically mobile activities.

1. Subject to final adoption of new legislation.
2. Also reviewed as a headquarters regime.
3. Also reviewed as a banking and insurance regime.
4. The regime has been abolished, however due to legal constraints the benefits of the regime remain available after 30 June 2021, beyond the agreed FHTP timelines.
5. Regime closed to new entrants on administrative basis and legal changes are forthcoming, which will be reviewed by the FHTP.

Table 2.9. Shipping regimes

	Jurisdiction	Regime	Status	Comments
1.	Antigua and Barbuda	Tonnage tax[1]	Not harmful (amended)	Ring-fencing removed. No grandfathering provided.
2.	Aruba	Shipping and aviation	Not harmful	No harmful features.
3.	Barbados	Shipping regime	Not harmful (amended)	Ring-fencing removed. No grandfathering provided.
4.	Hong Kong (China)	Profits tax exemptions for ship operators	Not harmful	No harmful features.
5.	Liberia	Shipping regime	Not harmful	No harmful features.
6.	Lithuania	Tonnage tax regime	Not harmful	No harmful features.
7.	Malta	Tonnage tax system	Not harmful	No harmful features.
8.	Mauritius	Shipping regime	Not harmful	No harmful features.
9.	Panama	Shipping regime	Not harmful	No harmful features.
10.	Singapore	Maritime sector incentive	Not harmful	No harmful features.

Note: The determination of substantial activity in the context of shipping regimes recognises that significant core income generating activities within shipping are performed in transit outside of the jurisdiction of the shipping regime, and that the value creation attributable to the core income generating activities that occur from a fixed location is more limited than for other types of regimes for mobile business income. The determination further considered whether the regime was designed to ensure that the qualifying taxpayer handles all corporate law and regulatory compliance of the shipping company with any additional obligations within the jurisdiction such as ship registration including compliance with International Maritime Organisation ("IMO") regulations, customs and manning requirements (noting the various regulatory requirements for shipping identified in the Consolidated Application Note) consistent with the IMO definition.

1. This regime will apply from 2021. The shipping regime under the Antigua and Barbuda Merchant Shipping Act 2006 has been abolished.

Table 2.10. Holding company regimes

	Jurisdiction	Regime	Status	Comments
1.	Andorra	Holding company regime	Not harmful (amended)	Ring-fencing removed. Grandfathering in accordance with FHTP timelines.
2.	Barbados	International societies with restricted liability	Abolished[1]	Grandfathering provided, see table note.
3.	Barbados	International trusts[2]	Abolished	No grandfathering provided.
4.	Saint Lucia	International trusts[3]	Abolished	Grandfathering in accordance with FHTP timelines.
5.	Saint Vincent and the Grenadines	International trusts[4]	Abolished	Grandfathering in accordance with FHTP timelines.

1. Subject to the confirmation of the closure of the grandfathered regime to new activities and new assets, which will be verified by the FHTP at the next opportunity.
2. Also reviewed as a financing and leasing regime.
3. Also reviewed as a financing and leasing regime.
4. Also reviewed as a financing and leasing regime.

Table 2.11. Fund management regimes

	Jurisdiction	Regime	Status	Comments
1.	Malaysia	Foreign fund management	Not harmful	No harmful features.

Table 2.12. Miscellaneous regimes

	Jurisdiction	Regime	Status	Comments
1.	Aruba	Investment promotion	Under review	Regime under review by FHTP.
2.	Aruba	IPC	Under review	Regime under review by FHTP.
3.	Aruba	San Nicolas	Abolished	Grandfathering in accordance with FHTP timelines.
4.	Barbados	Credit for foreign currency earnings / Credit for overseas project or services	Abolished	No grandfathering provided.
5.	Brunei Darussalam	Pioneer services companies	Under review	Regime under review by FHTP.
6.	Malaysia	Biotechnology industry	Not harmful (amended)	Substance requirements (non-IP) in place. Grandfathering in accordance with FHTP timelines.
7.	Malaysia	International currency business unit	Under review	Regime under review by FHTP.
8.	Malaysia	MSC Malaysia	Not harmful (amended)	Ring-fencing removed. Substance requirements (non-IP) in place. Grandfathering in accordance with FHTP timelines.
9.	Malaysia	Pioneer status – Contract R&D	Not harmful (amended)	Substance requirements (non-IP) in place. Grandfathering in accordance with FHTP timelines.
10.	Maldives	Reduced tax rates on profits sourced outside Maldives	In the process of being eliminated	Potentially harmful features will be addressed.
11.	Mauritius	Partial exemption system	Not harmful	New regime, designed in compliance with FHTP standards.
12.	Paraguay	Investment guarantee	Under review	Regime under review by FHTP.
13.	Paraguay	Investment of capital from abroad	Under review	Regime under review by FHTP.
14.	San Marino	New companies regime provided by art. 73, law no. 166/2013	Not harmful	No harmful features.
15.	San Marino	Regime for high-tech start-up companies under law no. 71/2013 and delegated decree no. 116/2014	Not harmful	No harmful features.
16.	Singapore	DEI-Legal services	Abolished	Grandfathering in accordance with FHTP timelines.
17.	Singapore	International growth scheme	Abolished	Grandfathering in accordance with FHTP timelines.
18.	United States	Foreign-derived intangible income (FDII)	Under review	Regime under review by FHTP.
19.	Uruguay	Benefits under law 16.906 for biotechnology	Not harmful (amended)	Substance requirements (non-IP) in place. No grandfathering provided.
20.	Uruguay	Benefits under lit S art. 52 for biotechnology and for software	Not harmful (amended)	Substance requirements (non-IP) in place. No grandfathering provided.
21.	Uruguay	Financial company reorganisation	Abolished	Regime abolished before FHTP assessment No grandfathering provided.

	Jurisdiction	Regime	Status	Comments
22.	Uruguay	Investment law incentives under law 16.096	Out of scope	No income from geographically mobile activities.
23.	Uruguay	Tax system according to the source principle	Out of scope	No divergence from the jurisdiction's general tax system.

References

OECD (2015), *Countering Harmful Tax Practices More Effectively, Taking into Account Transparency and Substance, Action 5 - 2015 Final Report*, OECD/G20 Base Erosion and Profit Shifting Project, OECD Publishing, Paris, https://dx.doi.org/10.1787/9789264241190-en. [1]

Chapter 3. Next steps

17.   The FHTP will continue to work on delivering a level playing field, including by ensuring substantial activities requirements are in place in no or only nominal tax jurisdictions. It will review newly identified regimes, monitor the changes made to date to ensure no new risks emerge, and consider the effectiveness of the criteria including whether revisions or additions are needed and more broadly work within the context of the Inclusive Framework to deliver outcomes that contribute to a fair and coherent international taxation framework.

18.   A significant deliverable in 2019 will be the review of the new global standard on the resumption of the substantial activities factor for no or only nominal tax jurisdictions. This will follow a similar approach to the process used for preferential regimes, evaluating the legal framework, having open discussion with the relevant jurisdictions, conducting monitoring of the implementation to ensure effectiveness in practice, and supplemented by specific spontaneous exchange of information. Further work will be undertaken in co-operation with Working Party 10 on Exchange of Information and Tax Compliance to develop the modalities and details for this spontaneous exchange of information. The Inclusive Framework will continue to report on the outcomes of this review process in due course, as it will do for preferential regimes.

19.   Furthermore, the FHTP conducts a yearly monitoring process in order to ensure if the implementation of certain aspects is in practice effectively meeting the standard. This occurs through standardised questionnaires, followed by a discussion in the FHTP with the relevant jurisdictions and an opportunity for the FHTP to reconsider its conclusion if necessary to ensure that the standards are met. The monitoring process takes place with respect to the following aspects:

- IP regimes (with respect to the granting of benefits to the third category of IP assets and the use of the rebuttable presumption[1]) (OECD, 2017[1]).

  Benefits granted to the third category of IP assets can only take place under certain conditions (e.g. it should contain a specific certification process and only small and medium enterprises can benefit). In addition, jurisdictions can only let taxpayers use the nexus approach as a rebuttable presumption in exceptional circumstances which should be demonstrated by the taxpayer. In both these circumstances, the FHTP conducts monitoring in order to ensure that the options are used appropriately.

- Potentially harmful but not actually harmful regimes[2] (OECD, 2017[1]).

  Where the FHTP concludes that a regime is potentially harmful but not actually harmful such a determination is based on statistical data, such as the number of taxpayers using the regime and the amount of income benefiting. However, this data may change and therefore the conclusion of "potentially but not actually harmful" is revisited as necessary.

- Disadvantaged areas regimes[3] (OECD, 2017[1]).

  Certain regimes are designed to encourage development in disadvantaged areas and may include a preferential rate for IP income, whilst they do not specifically provide for this. The FHTP concluded that such regimes do not pose a high risk of BEPS, provided certain conditions are met, and therefore the IP part of these regimes can be concluded as a "disadvantaged areas regime" which do not have to meet the requirement for the nexus approach. The FHTP monitors that the relevant conditions continue to be met.

- Substantial activities with respect to non-IP regimes reviewed in 2017 and thereafter.[4] (OECD, 2017[1]).

  The FHTP monitors whether the substantial activities requirements for these non-IP regimes are operating consistently with the legislative framework on which the finding of the FHTP was based, such as how taxpayer compliance is reviewed and how tax benefits are denied if substantial activities requirements are not met, together with relevant statistical data, including aggregate numbers of employees and income benefitting from the regime.

- Grandfathered non-IP regimes (OECD, 2017[1]).[5]

  Monitoring with respect to grandfathered non-IP regimes is conducted in order to ensure that jurisdictions are enforcing and implementing their grandfathering provisions in an effective way. The approach to this monitoring is contained in Annex B.

20.   The FHTP will also continue reviewing any preferential tax regimes that remain under review, any regimes of jurisdictions that join the Inclusive Framework going forward, and any additional "jurisdictions of relevance" as needed. In addition, it will review any newly introduced regimes.

Notes

[1] Paragraphs 37 and 69 of *Harmful Tax Practices - 2017 Progress Report on Preferential Regimes: Inclusive Framework on BEPS: Action 5* and Annex C of *Harmful Tax Practices - 2017 Progress Report on Preferential Regimes: Inclusive Framework on BEPS: Action 5*.

[2] Annex C of *Harmful Tax Practices - 2017 Progress Report on Preferential Regimes: Inclusive Framework on BEPS: Action 5*.

[3] Annex C of *Harmful Tax Practices - 2017 Progress Report on Preferential Regimes: Inclusive Framework on BEPS: Action 5*.

[4] Paragraphs 14-16 of Annex D of *Harmful Tax Practices - 2017 Progress Report on Preferential Regimes: Inclusive Framework on BEPS: Action 5*.

[5] Paragraph 27 of Annex B of *Harmful Tax Practices - 2017 Progress Report on Preferential Regimes: Inclusive Framework on BEPS: Action 5* and Annex B of this Progress Report.

References

OECD (2017), *Harmful Tax Practices - 2017 Progress Report on Preferential Regimes: Inclusive Framework on BEPS: Action 5*, OECD/G20 Base Erosion and Profit Shifting Project, OECD Publishing, Paris, https://dx.doi.org/10.1787/9789264283954-en. [1]

Annex A. Output of BEPS Action 5 mandate for considering revisions or additions to FHTP framework

1. Introduction

1.   The 1998 Report on Harmful Tax Competition: An Emerging Global Issue ("the 1998 Report" (OECD, 1998[1]) sets out the framework to identify harmful tax practices, with specific criteria for assessing harmful preferential regimes and for assessing "tax havens" (as they were then called).

2.   The criteria set out in the 1998 Report (OECD, 1998[1]) are still used by the Forum on Harmful Tax Practices ("FHTP") to determine whether a preferential regime within the scope of the FHTP's work is potentially harmful. This framework used four key factors and eight other factors. The four key factors were the following:

a) The regime imposes no or low effective tax rates on income from geographically mobile financial and other service activities.

b) The regime is ring-fenced from the domestic economy.

c) The regime lacks transparency (for example, the details of the regime or its application are not apparent, or there is inadequate regulatory supervision or financial disclosure).

d) There is no effective exchange of information with respect to the regime.

3.   The eight other factors were the following:

a) An artificial definition of the tax base.

b) Failure to adhere to international transfer pricing principles.

c) Foreign source income exempt from residence country taxation.

d) Negotiable tax rate or tax base.

e) Existence of secrecy provisions.

f) Access to a wide network of tax treaties.

g) The regime is promoted as a tax minimisation vehicle.

h) The regime encourages operations or arrangements that are purely tax-driven and involve no substantial activities.

4.   The criteria set out in the 1998 Report (OECD, 1998[1]) for assessing no or only nominal tax jurisdictions, a significant part of which is carried out by the Global Forum on Transparency and Exchange of Information for Tax Purposes, is:

a) whether a jurisdiction imposes no or only nominal taxes;

b) lack of effective exchange of information;

c) lack of transparency and

d) the absence of a requirement that the activity be substantial

5.	Action 5 of the BEPS Action Plan committed the FHTP to the following:

"Revamp the work on harmful tax practices with a priority on improving transparency, including compulsory spontaneous exchange on rulings related to preferential regimes, and on requiring substantial activity for any preferential regime. It will take a holistic approach to evaluate preferential tax regimes in the BEPS context. It will engage with non-OECD members on the basis of the existing framework and consider revisions or additions to the existing framework."

6.	The Action Plan specified that the FHTP would deliver the following three outputs: (i) finalisation of the review of OECD/G20 preferential regimes, (ii) a strategy to expand participation to non-OECD/non-G20 countries, and (iii) consideration of revisions or additions to the existing framework.

7.	As part of the first output, the FHTP elaborated both the substantial activities factor (the eighth other factor) and the transparency factor (the third key factor) over the course of the BEPS Project. The 2015 Final Report for Action 5 ("the 2015 Final Report") (OECD, 2015[2]) focused primarily on the first output, but the 2015 Final Report (OECD, 2015[2]) also briefly addressed the third output, regarding revision of criteria. The 2015 Final Report (OECD, 2015[2]) stated, "The OECD and G20 countries involved in the FHTP…consider that it is too early to accurately identify areas in which the existing criteria might fall short because the impact of the work on substance and transparency cannot yet be fully evaluated. In addition the benefits of involving third countries in this aspect of the work are recognised (OECD, 2015[2]).[1]"

8.	The 2015 Final Report (OECD, 2015[2]) then went on to discuss two factors "that could benefit from further consideration once the FHTP is better able to identify the impact of the other outputs considered in the 2015 Final Report (OECD, 2015[2])": the ring-fencing factor and the factor that focuses on "an artificial definition of the tax base (OECD, 2015[2]).[2]"

9.	Since the BEPS Action 5 Report (OECD, 2015) was published, the FHTP has discussed various approaches to revising the framework of the 1998 Report (OECD, 1998[1]).

10.	Consensus has been reached in the FHTP on a number of issues, including that it has been agreed to resume the substantial activities factor for no or only nominal tax jurisdictions. Given the speed at which jurisdictions with preferential regimes are making changes to their legal and administrative frameworks governing those regimes, and the importance of a level playing field, the outcome of that work was published immediately after approval, in November 2018. For convenience, it is reproduced herein.

11.	The FHTP also discussed additional issues relating to the scope of its work. This included whether a jurisdiction with a general no or low corporate tax rate could be considered harmful per se (without having regard to any of the other factors). In a similar vein, the FHTP also discussed whether a jurisdiction with a territorial tax system could be considered harmful per se, for example where the design of the source rules may facilitate double non-taxation, and whether territorial tax systems should be included in the scope of the new standard on substantial activities. The FHTP also considered whether its work should include preferential regimes that apply to the taxation of individuals as well as corporate taxation. The FHTP will continue its work on all relevant issues of harmful tax practices, such as the application of the no or low effective tax rate factor and whether further consideration is needed with respect to territorial tax systems, taking into account the ongoing work within the Inclusive Framework, including on the digital economy.

12.   The following table sets out the issues considered and the outcome. The issues are grouped according to: (i) substantive updates to the FHTP framework; and (ii) interpretive guidance on the application of existing factors for assessing regimes. The analysis of each issue is then described in detail below.

Table A.1. Substantive updates to the FHTP Framework

Issue	Outcome
Substantive updates to the FHTP Framework	
Updating the key factors in the 1998 Report for assessing regimes.	There are five key factors, including substantial activities as one of the key factors.
	The factor regarding access to a wide network of tax treaties is no longer useful for assessing regimes.
	The factor regarding promotion of a regime as a tax minimisation vehicle is no longer useful, in itself, for assessing regimes, although such promotion could prompt inquiry by reference to other factors.
The resumption of the application of the substantial activities factor for assessing no or only nominal tax jurisdictions.	The work on no or only nominal tax jurisdictions should be resumed, and the substantial activities criterion will be applied to those jurisdictions.
Interpretive guidance on the application of existing factors for assessing regimes	
The relationship between the key factors for assessing regimes and the other factors.	The other factors do not on their own indicate that a regime is potentially harmful, but provide evidence that one or more of the key factors may be met.
Whether other peer reviews related to transparency and exchange of information should inform the factors related to transparency and exchange of information.	To the extent that peer review results on the Action 5 transparency framework are relevant to the concerns underlying the transparency factor, they should be taken into account, but should not be determinative.
	The FHTP's transparency factor should not be modified to consider Global Forum peer review results regarding transparency.
	When assessing regimes under the exchange of information factor, the FHTP should consider Global Forum peer review results where relevant.
Whether the ring-fencing factor should be interpreted to include "de facto ring-fencing".	The ring fencing factor should not be modified to consider de facto ring-fencing, pursuant to which a preferential regime could be found to be ring-fenced due to a relatively small number of resident investors or beneficiaries in the regime even when the jurisdiction has no legal, administrative, or other implicit barriers to domestic investment.
Interpretation of ring-fencing considerations related to regimes that apply to transactions in foreign currency	A regime that only applies to transactions undertaken in foreign currency may not be considered ring-fenced if the regime otherwise permits residents to access the regime, the foreign currency in question is available to residents, is used as an alternative functional currency in the jurisdiction providing the regime and there are no exchange controls or other legal or practical limits that prevent resident taxpayers from entering into transactions in the currency that would qualify them for benefits under the regime.

2. Substantive updates to the FHTP framework

2.1. Updating the factors in the 1998 Report for assessing regimes

13.   As noted above, the 1998 Report (OECD, 1998[1]) contained four key factors, and eight other factors when reviewing preferential regimes. As part of the BEPS Project, two of the existing twelve factors were elaborated: the transparency factor (resulting in the minimum standard on compulsory spontaneous exchange of information on rulings) and the substantial activities factor. Given these changes, together with the experience gained in reviewing regimes in practice and other outcomes of the BEPS project, it was appropriate to reconsider some of the existing "other factors" and whether they were needed as separate elements.

14.   The role and relevance of three of the "other factors" contained in the 1998 Report (OECD, 1998[1]) have been considered: substantial activities; access to a wide network of tax treaties; and promotion of the regime as a tax minimisation vehicle.

15.   First, as part of the BEPS Project, the FHTP elevated the substantial activities factor. As such, the substantial activities factor has been elevated from being an "other factor" to a "key factor." In the context of IP regimes (which include any regime that provides benefits to income from any type of IP asset), this factor mandates that jurisdictions must provide no more benefits than those permitted under the nexus approach (OECD, 2015[2]).[3] In the context of non-IP regimes, the FHTP requires substantial activities whereby (1) jurisdictions must require core income generating activities to be performed and establish mechanisms to review compliance with this requirement, and (2) the FHTP will monitor the jurisdiction's effective implementation of the substantial activities requirement. In terms of the activities that jurisdictions must require, the FHTP agreed that jurisdictions must require taxpayers to have an adequate number of full-time employees with necessary qualifications and to incur an adequate amount of operating expenditures to undertake the core income-generating activities associated with the income that may benefit from a regime (OECD, 2017[3]).[4]

16.   Second, the factor relating to access to a wide network of tax treaties for assessing regimes was originally intended to prevent tax treaty abuse, but this factor does not in practice have any effect on tax treaty abuse. Furthermore, BEPS Action 6 has eliminated the need for this factor, given that it is one of the of BEPS minimum standards being implemented by members of the Inclusive Framework, and which is subject to a peer review. It was therefore concluded that this factor was no longer useful for assessing preferential regimes.

17.   Third, the factor relating to the regime being promoted as a tax minimisation vehicle is difficult to apply in practice. For example, ministerial publicity could rise to the level of government promotion in the eyes of some observers and not in the eyes of others. In addition, the use of this factor to assess a particular regime as harmful is difficult given that most jurisdictions promote their regimes in order to encourage the use of such regime, and determining whether such promotion was harmful in one case as opposed to another would be difficult and not likely to advance the discussion. It was concluded that this factor was no longer sufficiently useful, in itself, as a secondary factor, but that such promotion could prompt inquiry by reference to other factors.

18.   Given these changes, there are now *five* key factors for assessing regimes:

(i)   The regime imposes no or low effective tax rates on income from geographically mobile financial and other service activities.

    (ii) The regime is ring-fenced from the domestic economy.

    (iii) The regime lacks transparency.

    (iv) There is no effective exchange of information with respect to the regime.

    (v) The regime fails to require substantial activities.[5]

19.   The secondary factors are:

    (i) An artificial definition of the tax base.

    (ii) Failure to adhere to international transfer pricing principles.

    (iii) Foreign source income exempt from residence country taxation.

    (iv) Negotiable tax rate or tax base.

    (v) Existence of secrecy provisions.

2.2. *Resumption of application of substantial activities factor to no or only nominal tax jurisdictions*

Introduction

20.   The 1998 Report (OECD, 1998[1]) sets out a framework for approaching the problem of how certain no or only nominal tax jurisdictions ("tax havens" as they were then referred to in the 1998 Report (OECD, 1998[1]) and harmful preferential tax regimes "affect the location of financial and other service activities, erode the tax bases of other countries, distort trade and investment patterns and undermine the fairness, neutrality and broad social acceptance of tax systems (OECD, 1998[1]).[6]" The 1998 Report (OECD, 1998[1]) referred to certain no or only nominal tax jurisdictions and harmful preferential regimes collectively as "harmful tax practices," (although each discipline is mutually exclusive) and built a framework for how to assess these practices. There was a need to include both aspects of these practices, in order to deliver a level playing field between jurisdictions in a context where taxpayers can easily relocate their mobile activities in response to tax considerations.

21.   Given the elevation of the substantial activities requirement in the work on preferential regimes as part of the BEPS Project, it was appropriate to resume the application of the substantial activities requirement set out in the 1998 Report (OECD, 1998[1]) for no or only nominal tax jurisdictions and provide guidance on the application of the requirement.

Background

22.   The framework of the 1998 Report (OECD, 1998[1]) used for assessing preferential regimes used four key factors and eight other factors. The four key factors set out in the 1998 Report (OECD, 1998[1]) are the following:

a)   The regime imposes no or low effective tax rates on income from geographically mobile financial and other service activities.

b)   The regime is ring-fenced from the domestic economy.

c)   The regime lacks transparency (for example, the details of the regime or its application are not apparent, or there is inadequate regulatory supervision or financial disclosure).

d)   There is no effective exchange of information with respect to the regime.

23.   The corresponding framework for assessing whether a jurisdiction was a "tax haven" is based on four criteria: (a) whether a jurisdiction imposes no or only nominal

taxes; (b) lack of effective exchange of information; (c) lack of transparency and (d) the absence of a requirement that the activity be substantial (OECD, 1998[1]).[7]

24.   With regard to the substantial activities factor, the 1998 Report (OECD, 1998[1]) noted that "the absence of a requirement that the activity be substantial is important because it suggests that a jurisdiction may be attempting to attract investment and transactions that are purely tax driven. It may also indicate that a jurisdiction does not (or cannot) provide a legal or commercial environment or offer any economic advantages that would attract substantive business activities in the absence of the tax minimising opportunities it provides (OECD, 1998[1]).[8]" Notably, this is essentially the same rationale as applies in the case of preferential regimes.

25.   However, in 2001 the FHTP decided to only seek commitments and to determine whether or not a jurisdiction was considered uncooperative on the basis of the first three criteria.[9] This was followed by the release in 2002 of a list of uncooperative jurisdictions based on the first three criteria. The fourth criterion on substantial activities remained within the analytical framework of the work, but had no practical application.

26.   Subsequently, the Global Forum on Transparency and Exchange of Information for Tax Purposes grew out of the FHTP and took on the work on transparency and exchange of information, without distinction on the basis of tax rates or tax systems and with all jurisdictions participating on an equal basis. These developments meant that the FHTP's work then focussed on preferential regimes rather than no or only nominal tax jurisdictions.

27.   Therefore, until the BEPS Project, both of the frameworks in the 1998 Report (OECD, 1998[1]) (i.e., those on no or only nominal tax jurisdictions and on preferential regimes) included a criterion based on substantial activities, but in neither case was it in itself applied as a decisive factor for identifying, and eliminating, harmful tax practices.

28.   This changed with the creation of the BEPS Action Plan, which elevated the substantial activities requirement as it applied to preferential regimes, and the Inclusive Framework subsequently agreed guidance on what is required to meet this criterion[10] (OECD, 2017[3]). It is now an essential requirement, and without meeting this criterion a preferential regime that meets the gateway criterion and is within scope will be found to be potentially harmful. This now applies across the membership of the Inclusive Framework, which has grown to over 125 jurisdictions, and is a global standard.

29.   However, this leaves the analytical framework underlying the BEPS Action 5 work exposed to a potential incoherence: the substantial activities criterion has now been elevated as a key factor in one pillar of the work and is being applied, whereas it is not being applied in the other pillar of the work despite having been included as a key factor in the 1998 Report (OECD, 1998[1]) in that context.

30.   It also leaves the Inclusive Framework in a situation where, in elevating the substantial activities criteria for preferential regimes only, it has created a perceived level playing field issue. The specific concern that has been raised is that business could simply relocate to a no or only nominal tax jurisdiction to avoid having to meet the substance requirements that apply to preferential tax regimes. For example, some Inclusive Framework members which have a corporate income tax system offer international business company regimes, and these jurisdictions have been assessed and committed to amend or abolish the regimes. If the regime is being amended, this includes the addition of substantial activities requirements. At the same time, similar international business company laws apply in no or only nominal tax jurisdictions, but based on the current

application of the criteria, the Inclusive Framework would not ask for the same amendments or abolition of the corresponding legislation. It has been argued that this may even increase the pressure on taxing jurisdictions with low rates of corporate income tax to consider abolishing them – possibly triggering a race to the bottom that the FHTP was created to address.

31.   It was agreed to address this potential incoherence and address the perceived challenge to the level playing field, by drawing on the existing guidance agreed by the Inclusive Framework on the substantial activities factor that applies for preferential regimes. This would hold similar mobile business activities to a similar standard, irrespective of whether they are taxed under a preferential regime or a no or nominal tax rate.

32.   The resumption of the application of the substantial activities factor for assessing no or only nominal tax jurisdictions would address the particular level playing field challenges that have been raised, and recognise the particular risks that such jurisdictions create in attracting income without substantial local activities.

33.   However, this does not suggest that the absence of a corporate tax rate, or any particular level of corporate income tax is in itself harmful. This is analogous to the analytical framework for preferential regimes where the no or low effective tax rates criterion is a gateway criterion for the analysis of preferential regimes, but not in and of itself a harmful feature.

Translating the substantial activities requirements to a no or only nominal tax jurisdiction

Scope

34.   In order to translate the FHTP guidance on substantial activities to a no or only nominal tax jurisdiction, the starting point is to identify the jurisdictions to which it would apply. It would apply to jurisdictions which do not impose a corporate income tax. It would also apply to jurisdictions which impose only nominal corporate income tax to avoid the requirements.[11] It would not apply to jurisdictions which have been reviewed on the basis of the preferential regimes they offer (unless they subsequently significantly undertook reforms which abolished or substantially abolished their corporate income tax altogether).

35.   The next step is to identify the type of activities that are within the scope of the 1998 Report (OECD, 1998[1]). These are geographically mobile activities, such as financial and other service activities, including the provision of intangibles. The FHTP has typically identified these types of mobile activities as falling into the categories of headquarters, distribution centres, service centres, financing, leasing, fund management, banking, insurance, shipping, holding companies and the provision of intangibles.

36.   In respect of those activities, substantial activities requirements apply. The FHTP's guidance on substantial activities falls into two basic categories: activities earning non-IP income (which is set out in Annex D of the 2017 Progress Report (OECD, 2017[3])), and activities for the exploitation of IP assets (which is the nexus approach set out in the Action 5 Report (OECD, 2015[2])).

Non-IP income

37.   For activities within scope earning non-IP income, this would mean that the no or only nominal tax jurisdiction would be required to meet the same substantial activities

criterion (OECD, 2017[3]):,[12] meaning that it would need to introduce laws to (i) define the core income generating activities for each relevant business sector; (ii) ensure that core income generating activities relevant to the type of activity are undertaken by the entity (or are undertaken in the jurisdiction); (iii) require the entity to have an adequate number of full-time employees with necessary qualifications and incurring an adequate amount of operating expenditures to undertake such activities; and (iv) have a transparent mechanism to ensure compliance and provide an effective enforcement mechanism if these core income generating activities are not undertaken by the entity or do not occur within the jurisdiction.

38.	In order to implement these requirements in a context where there may be no corporate income tax that can be levied, and in some cases, no tax administration, a jurisdiction would need to implement rules that translate those requirements within the context of its legal and regulatory framework. Legislation may, for instance, be included in the financial services regulatory framework or the company incorporation framework.

IP income

39.	Where the business activities are the exploitation of IP assets, the substance requirements used by the FHTP are the "nexus approach". The nexus approach is essentially comprised of two elements: a first part which sets out a formula to determine the amount of eligible income which can benefit from a lower tax rate, and a second part which is a consequence for the non-eligible income which is then taxed at the normal (higher) tax rate. For a no or only nominal tax jurisdiction, the challenge is that even though the formula could be applied (the result of which might be that there is zero eligible income), it is unclear how to apply the second part.

40.	In other words, the nexus approach would clearly not function as intended because it is designed to operate within the context of a corporate income tax system. In such a system, the consequence of a taxpayer having income which does not qualify under the nexus formula (e.g. income earned from trademarks, or income earned where the IP has been acquired rather than developed by the entity) is the application of ordinary (non-preferential) corporate income tax rates to such income. This cannot translate by analogy to no or only nominal tax jurisdictions as there is no corporate income tax to impose.

41.	In order to translate the principle underlying the nexus approach to no or only nominal tax jurisdictions and deliver a level playing field, the best way forward is to apply a similar concept as applies for non-IP income, which is the core income generating activities guidance.

42.	At the outset, in all cases, the substantial activities requirements for IP income would always be insufficient if the entity only passively held IP assets which had been created and exploited on the basis of decisions made and activities performed outside of the jurisdiction. Similarly, the test would never be met if the only activities contributing to the income were the periodic decisions of non-resident board members in the jurisdiction.

IP income – patents and similar assets

43.	This would mean that if an entity is earning income from exploiting a patent (or similar IP assets as defined in paragraphs 34 – 37 of the Action 5 Report (OECD, 2015[2])), the entity should demonstrate that it has conducted the core income generating activities with the adequate number of qualified full-time employees and adequate amount of operating expenditures. The core income generating activities in this context would be conducting research and development (rather than simply acquiring or outsourcing it), which reflects the same concept as the nexus approach.

IP income – marketing intangibles

44.　An adjustment would be needed from the nexus approach where an entity is exploiting marketing IP assets such as trademarks.[13] The nexus approach provides that this type of IP asset is not permitted to benefit from a preferential regime, given that the policy rationale of an IP regime is to encourage and reward scientific innovation rather than marketing activity, with the consequence that a taxpayer engaged in exploiting marketing intangibles is required to pay tax at the ordinary rate. However, in the context of a no or only nominal tax jurisdiction, there is no (or no significant) "ordinary" tax to apply. An analogous approach would be to apply a similar substantial activities principle as set out in the preceding paragraph, where the core income generating activities are branding, marketing, and distribution.

IP income – exceptional cases and rebuttable presumption

45.　It is possible that an entity exploiting IP assets in a no or only nominal tax jurisdiction could in fact be conducting substantial activities, even if this did not involve research and development (for patents and similar assets) or branding, marketing and distribution (for marketing IP assets). Although such situations should be the exception rather than the rule, there may be some situations where it will be appropriate to give the entity some flexibility to demonstrate that it is performing the core income generating activities with the adequate number of qualified full-time employees and adequate amount of operating expenditures. Such activities could include conducting the strategic decision-making, managing and bearing the principal risks relating to the development and subsequent exploitation of the IP asset, or carrying on the underlying trading activities through which the asset is exploited.

46.　However, as the absence of substantial activities in the form of research and development, or marketing, branding, and distribution (as the case may be depending on the type of IP asset) creates additional risks, the ability to conduct other types of activities and still meet the substantial activities test should be prima facie excluded for higher risk scenarios.

47.　Higher risk scenarios would be cases where (i) the entity has acquired the IP asset from related parties or through the entity funding research and development activities which took place outside the no or only nominal tax jurisdiction; and (ii) the IP asset is licensed or sold to related parties, or the exploitation is conducted by related parties outside the jurisdiction (e.g. foreign related parties are paid to develop and sell a product in which the intangible asset is embedded).

48.　In these higher risk scenarios, there should be a "rebuttable presumption" that the substantial activities test is not met in the absence of research and development (for patent and similar IP assets), or in the absence of marketing, branding, and distribution (for marketing intangibles). This would be the case notwithstanding that a transfer pricing analysis would allocate some profits to the entity.

49.　However, similar to the rebuttable presumption created in BEPS Action 5 in the context of the nexus approach, a company in a higher risk scenario could rebut the presumption, by providing evidence that the income generated is directly linked to activities undertaken in the local jurisdiction rather than in a foreign jurisdiction.

50.   Given the risks, this would need to be a high evidential threshold. Entities would need to provide evidence that there was, and historically has been, a high degree of control over the development, enhancement, maintenance, protection and exploitation of the intangible asset, exercised by an adequate number of full-time employees with the necessary qualifications that permanently reside and perform their activities within the jurisdiction. This would need to be demonstrated by providing additional information including:

- detailed business plans which demonstrate the commercial rationale for holding the IP assets in the jurisdiction;

- employee information, including level of experience, type of contracts, qualifications, and duration of employment; and

- evidence that decision making is taking place within the jurisdiction, rather than periodic decisions of non-resident board members.

51.   In keeping with the agreed approach for certain aspects of the nexus approach, this rebuttable presumption would be subject to a review by the FHTP no later than 2020.

52.   A graphic providing an overview of the requirements as they apply for IP income is included in Table A.2.

Table A.2. Application of substance requirements for IP income

Lower risk scenarios				Higher risk scenarios (i.e. involvement of foreign related parties)			
1. IP assets (e.g. patents) *Substantial activity = R&D*	+ Necessary staff, premises, equipment, expenditure, decision-making etc.	+ **Filing information** Type A. Business type, gross income, expenses and assets, premises, employees, proof of core income generating activities, etc.	= ✓	1. IP assets (e.g. patents) *Substantial activity = R&D*	+ Necessary staff, premises, equipment, expenditure, decision-making etc.	+ **Filing information** Type A. Business type, gross income, expenses and assets, premises, employees, proof of core income generating activities, etc.	= ✓
2. Marketing assets (e.g. trademarks) *Substantial activity = branding, marketing and distribution*	+ Necessary staff, premises, equipment, expenditure, decision-making etc.	+ **Filing information** Type A. Business type, gross income, expenses and assets, premises, employees, proof of core income generating activities, etc.	= ✓	2. Marketing assets (e.g. trademarks) *Substantial activity = branding, marketing and distribution*	+ Necessary staff, premises, equipment, expenditure, decision-making etc.	+ **Filing information** Type A. Business type, gross income, expenses and assets, premises, employees, proof of core income generating activities, etc.	= ✓
3. Other Core Income Generating Activities (CIGA) *Substantial activity = Strategic decision-making, managing and bearing principal risks, underlying trading activities, etc.*	+ Necessary staff, premises, equipment, expenditure, decision-making etc.	+ **Filing information** Type A. Business type, gross income, expenses and assets, premises, employees, proof of core income generating activities, etc.	= ✓	3. Other Core Income Generating Activities (CIGA) *Substantial activity =* - High degree of DEMPE; and - Historical DEMPE; and - Full time highly skilled employees that permanently reside and perform CIGA in the no or only nominal tax jurisdiction	+ Necessary staff, premises, equipment, expenditure, decision-making etc.	+ **Filing information** Type A information *PLUS* Type B information - Detailed business plans; - Employee information; - Proof of decision-making in jurisdiction	= ✓

Scenarios which are not sufficient to meet substance requirements for IP income

4. Merely passively holding the IP asset in the jurisdiction	=	✖
5. Periodic decisions of non-resident board members	=	✖

Ensuring compliance

53.   A key element of the substantial activities requirements is that there is an effective mechanism to ensure compliance. In the context of a taxing jurisdiction offering a preferential regime, this can be done, for example, by collecting information in tax returns, and denying tax benefits to the extent the requirements are not met. As this does not apply in the context of a no or only nominal tax jurisdiction, other approaches are needed to provide an equivalent means to ensure compliance.

54.   First, there should be a mechanism to identify the entities conducting the relevant categories of mobile activities and to detect whether the core income generating activities were being carried out. To be able to do so, the relevant entities would need to report information in the jurisdiction on:

- the type of mobile activity being conducted;

- the relevant core income generating activities the entity has conducted;

- the amount and type of gross income (e.g. rents, royalties, dividends, sales, services);

- the amount and type of expenses incurred, and assets and premises held, in the course of carrying out the business; and

- the number of full-time, qualified employees.

55.   Second, there should be a mechanism to take action in the event an entity failed to meet the substantial activities requirements. Given that there is no ability to apply a higher rate of tax as would be the case in the context of a preferential regime, there should be a sanction mechanism that is rigorous, effective and dissuasive. The determination of whether a sanction mechanism is rigorous, effective, and dissuasive will depend on the context. If relevant and appropriate, such a mechanism would include striking an entity off the register where this is an effective sanction. The no or only nominal tax jurisdiction would also need to continue enforcement efforts and remedy any shortcomings in the enforcement process.

56.   Third, there should also be the following enhanced spontaneous exchange of information of the information filed with the jurisdiction based on, subject to and limited by the applicable exchange of information instruments. The framework for spontaneous exchange of information will consist of two parts. First, for any entities that do not comply with the substantial activities requirement, all no or nominal tax jurisdictions would be required to spontaneously exchange all relevant information with the jurisdictions of residence of the immediate parent, ultimate parent, and ultimate beneficial owner.

57.   Furthermore, outside the context of non-compliant entities, the scope of further spontaneous exchange will depend on whether a no or nominal tax jurisdiction can demonstrate that it has a fully equipped monitoring process. This means a monitoring process operated by a tax administration or other governmental authority with all resources, processes and procedures in place to ensure not only an effective data collection process but also a high-quality review of the substantial activities standard with proactive follow-up where necessary. The FHTP will determine whether monitoring mechanisms are equipped with the appropriate resources and effective processes and procedures.

58.   If a jurisdiction does demonstrate that it has a fully equipped monitoring process, it would only be required to spontaneously exchange information on entities engaged in

high-risk scenarios, as defined in paragraph 34. In such scenarios, the exchange would be a two-step process. The first step would be the annual exchange of the name and address of the entity; the type of mobile income; the name of the immediate parent, ultimate parent and ultimate beneficial owner; and the amount and type of gross income (e.g. rents, royalties, dividends, sales, services). In the second step, the recipient jurisdiction could then make a follow up request for further information, subject to the applicable exchange of information instrument.

59.   If a jurisdiction does not demonstrate that it has a fully equipped monitoring mechanism, it would be required to spontaneously exchange all relevant information on entities engaged in high-risk scenarios, as defined in paragraph 34. For all other entities conducting activities in scope, as set out in paragraph 22, the jurisdiction would be required to use the two-step exchange process described in paragraph 45.

60.   All exchanges would provide information to the jurisdictions of residence of the immediate parent, ultimate parent, and ultimate beneficial owner.

61.   The tables on the next pages set out the different types of information to be exchanged in different scenarios.

Table A.3. Jurisdictions with fully equipped monitoring mechanisms

Scenario requiring exchange	Content of exchange	Recipient jurisdictions
Non-compliance by the entity	<ul><li>Entity name and address</li><li>Summary of what elements of the core income generating activities test the entity has failed to meet</li><li>Name of the immediate parent, ultimate parent, and ultimate beneficial owner</li><li>Type of mobile income</li><li>Amount and type of gross income</li><li>Amount and type of expenses incurred, and assets and premises held, in the course of carrying out the business</li><li>Number of full-time, qualified employees</li><li>Any other relevant information.</li></ul>	Residence jurisdictions of:<ul><li>Immediate parent</li><li>Ultimate parent</li><li>Ultimate beneficial owner</li></ul>
In high risk cases (see paragraph 34) that are not also cases of non-compliance by the entity	*Step 1:* annual exchange of:<ul><li>Entity name and address</li><li>Type of mobile income</li><li>Name of the immediate parent, ultimate parent, and ultimate beneficial owner</li><li>Amount and type of gross income (e.g. rents, royalties, dividends, sales, services)</li></ul>*Step 2:* recipient jurisdiction makes follow up request for further information	Residence jurisdictions of:<ul><li>Immediate parent</li><li>Ultimate parent</li><li>Ultimate beneficial owner</li></ul>

Table A.4. Jurisdictions without fully equipped monitoring mechanisms

Scenario requiring exchange	Content of exchange	Recipient jurisdictions
Non-compliance by the entity and in high-risk cases (see paragraph 34)	• Entity name and address • Summary of what elements of the core income generating activities test the entity has failed to meet (for non-compliant entities) • Summary of the core income generating activities performed by the entity (for high-risk scenarios) • Name of the immediate parent, ultimate parent, and ultimate beneficial owner • Type of mobile income • Amount and type of gross income • Amount and type of expenses incurred, and assets and premises held, in the course of carrying out the business • Number of full-time, qualified employees • Any other relevant information.	Residence jurisdictions of: • Immediate parent • Ultimate parent • Ultimate beneficial owner
In all other cases involving entities engaged in activities within scope (see paragraph 22)	*Step 1*: annual exchange of: • Entity name and address • Type of mobile income • Name of the immediate parent, ultimate parent, and ultimate beneficial owner • Amount and type of gross income (e.g. rents, royalties, dividends, sales, services) *Step 2*: recipient jurisdiction makes follow up request for further information	Residence jurisdictions of: • Immediate parent • Ultimate parent • Ultimate beneficial owner

62.	To activate the exchanges set out above, recipient jurisdictions would need to opt in to receive spontaneously exchanged information.

63.	The modalities of the above exchange framework, including the terminology used in the framework, timing for such exchanges, the precise data points, the details of what constitutes a fully equipped monitoring mechanism, the mechanism for opting in, and the development of a standardised template and XML schema, will be developed in cooperation with Working Party 10, drawing also on other reporting regimes, in 2019 and prior to the first exchanges under the framework.

64.	To ensure the effectiveness of the information collection and exchange mechanism, a review will take place in 2022 in cooperation with Working Party 10, which should provide enough time to allow jurisdictions to gain experience with the mechanism. Should particular issues surface in the operation of the exchange mechanism, the FHTP could also have an earlier discussion.

3. Interpretive guidance on the application of existing factors for assessing regimes

3.1. Introduction

65.	This second part provides interpretive guidance on applying the factors in the review of preferential regimes. This relates to: the relationship between the key factors and other factors and how the secondary factors can inform the key factors; guidance on interpreting transparency and exchange of information factors; and guidance on the ring-fencing factor, relating to de-facto ring-fencing and foreign currency regimes.

3.2. The relationship between the key factors for assessing regimes and the other factors

66.   The first key factor must be met in order for the FHTP's analysis of a regime's harmfulness to continue. If any one of the following four key factors is also met, then the regime will be found to be potentially harmful.

67.   When determining whether the five key factors are present, the FHTP may consider any relevant information, but several secondary factors could be particularly relevant. These factors do not on their own indicate that a regime is potentially harmful, but they provide evidence that one or more of the key factors may be met. The subsections below outline both the relevant secondary factors to be considered and further areas related to the key factors. The examples included therein are illustrative. The FHTP may consider the secondary factors in the context of any of the key factors, and one secondary factor may be relevant to more than one key factor.

Consideration of whether a regime imposes no or low effective tax rates

68.   In considering whether a regime imposes no or low tax rates, the FHTP may consider the following secondary factors:

- An artificial definition of the tax base: The 1998 Report and the Consolidated Application Note (CAN) both make clear that the first key factor considers effective tax rates as well as statutory rates. Therefore, consideration of how the tax base is defined is appropriate when determining the effective tax rate.

- Negotiable tax rate or tax base: The 1998 Report and the CAN both make clear that the first key factor considers effective tax rates as well as statutory rates. Therefore, consideration of whether the tax rate or tax base is open for negotiation is appropriate when determining the effective tax rate.

- Failure to adhere to international transfer pricing principles: The CAN makes clear that failure to adhere to international transfer pricing principles is likely to arrive at a different tax base with respect to intra-group transactions which may result in a lowering of the tax base and therefore of the effective tax rate.

Consideration of whether a regime is ring-fenced

69.   In considering whether a regime is ring-fenced, the FHTP may consider the following secondary factor:

- Foreign source income exempt from residence country taxation: The 1998 Report (OECD, 1998[1]) states that this secondary factor is to be considered because "[a] country that exempts all foreign-source income from tax, i.e., the regime is a territorial system, may be particularly attractive since the exemption reduces the effective income tax rate and encourages the location of activities for tax rather than business purposes. Since entities which take advantage of these regimes can be used as conduits or to engage in treaty shopping, they may have harmful effects on other countries." However, the CAN (OECD, 2004[4]) notes that no case of ring fencing arises with respect to measures that are part of a jurisdiction's general system of taxation or if the non-taxation of foreign source income is a measure designed to eliminate or mitigate double taxation, as set out in paragraphs 243-244 of the CAN (OECD, 2004[4]).[14] Consistent with the 1998 Report, the secondary factor on exempt foreign income can inform consideration of whether a particular regime is ring-fenced.

- Failure to adhere to international transfer pricing principles: The CAN makes clear that this factor may indicate ring-fencing, where benefits available under a transfer pricing regime are explicitly or implicitly restricted to foreign-owned enterprises or if taxpayers benefiting from the regime and associated enterprises abroad were treated in a more beneficial way than similar transactions with associated enterprises in the domestic market.

Consideration of whether a regime lacks transparency

70.　In assessing whether there is a lack of transparency, the FHTP may consider the following secondary factors:

- Failure to adhere to international transfer pricing principles: the 1998 Report notes that the inconsistent or negotiable application of transfer pricing rules can be non-transparent (e.g. where the principles for the allocation of income are not clearly stipulated in the laws and regulations or where an individual taxpayer can negotiate a transfer price with the tax authorities). Therefore, the absence of rules requiring consistent application of transfer pricing rules may inform consideration of whether a regime lacks transparency.

- Negotiable tax rate or tax base: where a taxpayer can negotiate the rate or base within a preferential regime, this may give rise to concern that the regime is not transparent.

Consideration of whether there is no effective exchange of information

71.　In assessing whether there is no effective exchange of information, the FHTP may consider the following secondary factor:

- Existence of secrecy provisions: No revisions to this secondary factor are needed, but it may inform the determination of whether the exchange of information factor is met.

Summary

72.　Examples of how the secondary factors can inform the key factors are:

(i) An artificial definition of the tax base. This secondary factor can inform determinations of whether the key factors are met, including whether a regime imposes no or low effective tax rates.

(ii) Failure to adhere to international transfer pricing principles. This secondary factor can inform determinations of whether a regime imposes no or low effective tax rates, whether a regime is ring-fenced, and whether a regime fails to meet the transparency factor.

(iii) Foreign source income exempt from residence country taxation. This secondary factor can inform determinations of whether the key factors are met, including whether a regime is ring-fenced.

(iv) Negotiable tax rate or tax base. This secondary factor can inform determinations of whether the key factors are met, including whether a regime imposes no or low effective tax rates and lacks transparency.

(v) Existence of secrecy provisions. This secondary factor can inform determinations of whether the key factors are met, including whether a regime lacks exchange of information.

3.3. Additional guidance on interpreting transparency and exchange of information factors

73.   The Action 5 minimum standard has already revised what the FHTP must take into account when assessing whether a regime lacks transparency with respect to rulings. In the context of a regime that provides a ruling, information on the ruling must be spontaneously exchanged as required by the Action 5 Final Report (OECD, 2015[2]) (the "transparency framework").[15]

74.   It was also discussed whether the FHTP should take peer review results regarding a country's compliance with the transparency framework into account when determining whether a regime lacks transparency. It was agreed that, to the extent that these peer review results are relevant to the concerns underlying the transparency factor, they should be considered but should not be determinative.

75.   However, with respect to the peer reviews on exchange of information on request carried out by the Global Forum on Transparency and Exchange of information for Tax Purposes ("Global Forum") the transparency factor from the 1998 Report (OECD, 1998[1]) focuses on the legal and administrative operation of a regime, which is fundamentally different than the transparency considered by Global Forum peer reviews, which consider transparency in the context of the availability of information (bank, ownership, identity and accounting), that tax authorities can access and have a legal basis to exchange with another tax authority. It was therefore concluded that the Global Forum peer review ratings, to the extent that they did contain any relevant information for the transparency factor, should be taken into account, but cannot be determinative for assessing a regime under the transparency factor.

76.   However, it would be reasonable to assume that a negative peer review could be symptomatic of a jurisdiction's deficiencies in areas such as exchange of information and it would seem counterintuitive to disregard the results of Global Forum peer reviews entirely when applying the exchange of information factor. It was therefore concluded that Global Forum peer reviews should be considered in assessing the exchange of information factor for preferential tax regimes where relevant.

3.4. Additional guidance on ring-fencing

De facto ring-fencing

77.   The issue of whether this factor should be regarded as applying where a regime is "de facto ring-fenced" because only a small number of resident taxpayers in fact take advantage of the regime was also considered.

78.   Ring-fencing occurs when a regime is "partially or fully isolated from the domestic economy."[16] As will be outlined in the following paragraphs, de facto ring-fencing is not included in the definition of ring-fencing in the 1998 Report (OECD, 1998[1]) or subsequent reports or guidance.

79.   The 1998 Report (OECD, 1998[1]) considered two versions of ring-fencing. In the first version, a regime would "explicitly or implicitly exclude resident enterprises from taking advantage of their benefits". In the second version, "investors who benefit from the tax regime are explicitly or implicitly denied access to domestic markets."[17] Both of these versions focus on legal or administrative barriers, either to residents who attempt to use the regime or to non-residents who attempt to access the domestic market. The 1998 Report (OECD, 1998[1]) did, however, mention that the second version of ring-fencing

could include implicit denial of market access. In discussing this possibility, the 1998 Report (OECD, 1998[1]) stated, "Market access may be denied on a de-facto basis through special tax privileges not applying or being otherwise neutralised insofar as the enterprises carry on business in the regime-country's domestic market." Although this statement uses the term "de facto," it is focused only on de facto neutralisation of benefits to certain investors, *not* on a small number of resident taxpayers taking advantage of the regime even though they have access to the benefits under the regime. It is therefore focused on *implicit* ring-fencing, whereby legal or administrative barriers prevent access to the domestic market, but they do so less explicitly than legal barriers that on their face limit access to resident taxpayers. This discussion of implicit ring-fencing does not address de facto ring-fencing, where there are no legal barriers preventing access but there are instead only a small number of resident taxpayers who benefit from the regime.

80.	Therefore, *explicit ring-fencing* occurs when a regime by its own terms excludes access to resident taxpayers or to the domestic market. *Implicit ring-fencing* occurs when a regime does not exclude access to resident taxpayers or the domestic market in the letter of the law but instead through administrative or legal barriers that prohibit or inhibit resident taxpayers or domestic market participants from benefiting from the regime. *De facto ring-fencing*, in contrast, would occur when, even in the absence of any administrative or legal barriers, resident taxpayers still make up only a small percentage of the taxpayers benefiting from the regime.

81.	To clarify this distinction between *implicit* ring-fencing, which is already included in the definition of impermissible ring-fencing, and *de facto* ring-fencing, which is not, consider two examples. First, consider a regime that by its terms is available to all qualifying taxpayers but where the administrative practice of the jurisdiction has the effect of limiting the regime to foreign taxpayers. This regime is implicitly ring-fenced, and it would already be included in the definition of ring-fencing as defined by the 1998 Report (OECD, 1998[1]) and the CAN. Second, consider a regime that by its terms is available to all qualifying taxpayers and where the jurisdiction does nothing administratively to limit this regime to foreign taxpayers. In practice, however, the regime is provided by a jurisdiction with a relatively small economy, so the majority of taxpayers that can benefit from the regime are foreign taxpayers. Even if every possible qualifying resident taxpayer benefits from the regime, the jurisdiction's population and economy mean that resident taxpayers only make up a minority of beneficiaries. This situation is not included in the definition of ring-fencing, but it illustrates the type of de facto ring-fencing that certain jurisdictions proposed including in the definition of ring-fencing.

82.	The fact that the 1998 Report (OECD, 1998[1]) does not include the type of de facto ring-fencing proposed by delegates in its definition of ring-fencing is made explicit in the CAN, which states that:

> "a mere absence of domestic operators in the preferred sector or the absence of an existing domestic market for the services qualifying for the preferential regime *does not constitute ring-fencing*. There must be a deliberate legal restriction, or other restriction with similar effect, on access to the domestic market, i.e., access must be denied or residents must be excluded from taking advantage of the preferential regime. What is at issue, therefore, is whether there are measures that a country takes to protect itself from the potentially harmful effects of its own preferential regime and not a requirement that there should be a domestic market or domestic users for the preferred activities. In short, *the 1998 Report is not concerned with situations where enterprises qualifying for a preferential regime*

are permitted to operate in the domestic market but in practice do not. (OECD, 2004[4])."[18]

83.   In considering whether to expand the definition of ring-fencing to include de facto ring-fencing several practical issues arise.

84.   First, including de facto ring-fencing in the second factor would require a definition of this term, which in turn raises significant questions. For instance, how low must resident investment be in order to be treated as de facto ring-fencing? Should the percentage of resident investors be proportional to the portion of the world population in the country in question, or to the portion of world GDP in the country in question, or to some other comparable ratio? Or should there be a set number below which domestic investment cannot fall, or else there will be a finding of de facto ring-fencing?

85.   Second, finding regimes to be ring-fenced due to a low number of resident investors would be likely to affect only smaller countries with high rates of foreign investment, and such an approach would be likely to affect all the regimes of those countries, whether or not they are in fact harmful. Additionally, focusing on the percentage of resident investors in a regime would not determine whether the regime is isolated from the domestic economy. It could instead reveal that the domestic economy has a limited number of investors able to benefit from the regime or that the domestic economy is dependent on foreign investors. Neither of these general characteristics of an economy would automatically mean that all regimes in that economy were potentially harmful, but a definition of ring-fencing that includes de facto ring-fencing would lead to just such a finding.

86.   Third, basing a decision on the extent to which resident taxpayers make use of a regime could result in a situation where identical regimes in different countries would be treated differently by the FHTP solely because there was significant domestic use of the incentive in one country but not in the other.

87.   Fourth, examining regimes for de facto ring-fencing based on domestic use of the incentive would also suggest that there would need to be ongoing monitoring of all regimes which the FHTP determines not to be ring-fenced in order to verify that domestic use of the incentive remained significant enough to conclude that the regime continued not to be de facto ring-fenced. It is nevertheless true that the FHTP engages in ongoing monitoring already. Therefore, this particular issue may be most relevant to considerations of burden on tax administrations and certainty for taxpayers benefitting from preferential regimes.

88.   Therefore, it was agreed not to expand the definition of ring-fencing to include de facto ring-fencing. However, the FHTP can consider the relative number of resident taxpayers benefiting from a regime as an indicator of whether further inquiry is necessary to identify whether there are administrative or legal barriers that would amount to implicit ring-fencing. This does not change the definition of ring-fencing to mean that a relatively small number of resident taxpayers leads to a conclusion that a regime has been ring-fenced.

Foreign currency regimes

89.   A further ring-fencing issue that arose was whether a regime that provides benefits only to transactions carried out in a foreign currency can ever be considered not to be ring-fenced. The 1998 Report clearly lists as an example of ring-fencing a situation where "the regime may not permit transactions in the domestic currency, thus ensuring

that the domestic monetary system is not affected by the regime. (OECD, 1998[1])"[19] The CAN (OECD, 2004[4]) supports this conclusion, stating that one example of ring-fencing "would be cases where the ability to operate domestically is restricted, or made more cumbersome, through the requirement that entities qualifying under the regime do business only in foreign denominated currencies. (OECD, 2004[4])"[20]

90.   There is therefore no question that a regime that requires that transactions be undertaken in a foreign currency is on its face ring-fenced from the domestic market. Some jurisdictions, however, questioned whether there could be a policy exception for such regimes if the regimes were designed not to attract investment but instead to attract foreign currency in order to address balance of payments concerns. In order for such a regime to be consistent with the requirements of the 1998 Report (OECD, 1998[1]) and the CAN (OECD, 2004[4]), it seems that foreign currency would have to be accessible to domestic residents and used as an alternative functional currency in the jurisdiction providing the regime. If the foreign currency were in general circulation throughout the domestic economy and there were no legal or practical limits on resident taxpayers accessing that foreign currency, then a regime that applied only to transactions in that foreign currency would be less likely to be seen as ring-fenced. Such regimes would need to be assessed by the FHTP on a case-by-case basis. If, however, resident taxpayers were not easily able to use the foreign currency, then such a regime would have the practical effect of applying only to foreign transactions, which would lead to a conclusion that it was ring-fenced. For example, a jurisdiction may have legal limitations that prohibit resident taxpayers from accessing foreign currency, or practical limitations that require resident taxpayers to automatically convert all or a portion of foreign currency they receive into the domestic currency, or a requirement that the approval of the central bank be obtained in order to convert domestic currency into foreign currency, thereby hampering their free access to foreign currency.

91.   It was concluded that the definition of ring-fencing includes regimes that apply only to transactions in foreign currencies, but that such regimes may not be ring-fenced if:

- the regime otherwise permits residents to access the regime;

- the foreign currency in question is available to residents;

- the foreign currency is in general circulation throughout the domestic economy such that the foreign currency is effectively used as an alternative functional currency in the jurisdiction providing the regime; and

- there are no exchange controls or other legal or practical limits that prevent resident taxpayers from entering into transactions in the currency that would qualify them for benefits under the regime.

92.   Such regimes will be assessed by the FHTP on a case-by-case basis.

Notes

[1] Para. 155.

[2] Para. 156-158.

[3] For a detailed description of the nexus approach as applied to IP regimes, see *Countering Harmful Tax Practices More Effectively, Taking into Account Transparency and Substance, Action 5 - 2015 Final Report*, pp. 24-36.

[4] For a detailed description of the substantial activities requirements as applied to all other regimes, see *Countering Harmful Tax Practices More Effectively, Taking into Account Transparency and Substance, Action 5 - 2015 Final Report*, pp. 39-44.

[5] This includes the OECD reports *Countering Harmful Tax Practices More Effectively, Taking into Account Transparency and Substance, Action 5 - 2015 Final Report, Harmful Tax Practices - 2017 Progress Report on Preferential Regimes: Inclusive Framework on BEPS: Action 5*, and any guidance on substantial activities agreed by the FHTP and Inclusive Framework thereafter.

[6] Para. 4.

[7] Para. 52.

[8] Para. 55.

[9] This decision was driven in large part by technical challenges in applying the criteria, and the fact that at the time the jurisdictions affected by it were not participants in the work. Both of these aspects are significantly different now from what they were then, given the agreed guidance on substantial activities in preferential regimes, and the institutional changes brought by the Inclusive Framework.

[10] See Annex D of *Harmful Tax Practices - 2017 Progress Report on Preferential Regimes: Inclusive Framework on BEPS: Action 5*.

[11] *Harmful Tax Competition: An Emerging Global Issue* uses the terminology of "no or low effective tax rates" for preferential regimes and "no or only nominal taxes" for jurisdictions that were then called "tax havens" without defining either term by reference to a set or a specific rate. The purpose of considering nominal tax jurisdictions along with zero tax jurisdictions is to ensure that there is not an incentive for zero rate jurisdictions to shift to a rate near zero.

[12] Within the non-IP income category, there is specific guidance that applies given the nature of pure equity holding companies and shipping activities. For holding companies, see paragraph 8 of Annex D of *Harmful Tax Practices - 2017 Progress Report on Preferential Regimes: Inclusive Framework on BEPS: Action 5*. For shipping companies see note 1 under the table of results on shipping regimes in Chapter 2 of the Progress Report.

[13] The normal rule under the nexus approach, whereby marketing-related IP assets such as trademarks cannot qualify for tax benefits, remains unchanged. However, there is a difficulty in applying the nexus approach to no or only nominal tax jurisdictions. Under the nexus approach, the preferential tax treatment cannot apply to income from such assets and instead tax is to be paid at the ordinary rate. However, in the case of no or only nominal tax jurisdictions, there is no preferential rate and no ordinary rate to apply where income from such assets is earned. The application of the nexus rule would mean as a matter of law or otherwise that entities in a no or only nominal tax jurisdiction would not be allowed to hold and receive returns on marketing intangibles at all. This would seem disproportionate.

[14] Consolidated Application Note: Guidance in Applying the 1998 Report to Preferential Tax Regimes (hereafter "CAN"), paras. 243-244.

[15] See chapter 5 of *Harmful Tax Practices - 2017 Progress Report on Preferential Regimes: Inclusive Framework on BEPS: Action 5.*

[16] *Harmful Tax Competition: An Emerging Global Issue* (hereafter "1998 Report), para. 62.

[17] *Harmful Tax Competition: An Emerging Global Issue*, para 62. The 1998 Report also briefly identified a third version of ring-fencing: a regime where transactions are not permitted in the domestic currency. See discussion in paragraphs 77 - 80.

[18] Consolidated Application Note: Guidance in Applying the 1998 Report to Preferential Tax Regimes (hereafter "CAN"), paragraph 68 (emphasis added).

[19] 1998 Report, para 62.

[20] CAN, para 76.

References

OECD (2017), *Harmful Tax Practices - 2017 Progress Report on Preferential Regimes: Inclusive Framework on BEPS: Action 5*, OECD/G20 Base Erosion and Profit Shifting Project, OECD Publishing, Paris, https://dx.doi.org/10.1787/9789264283954-en. [3]

OECD (2015), *Countering Harmful Tax Practices More Effectively, Taking into Account Transparency and Substance, Action 5 - 2015 Final Report*, OECD/G20 Base Erosion and Profit Shifting Project, OECD Publishing, Paris, https://dx.doi.org/10.1787/9789264241190-en. [2]

OECD (2004), *Consolidated Application Note - Guidance in applying the 1998 report to preferential tax regimes*, OECD, Paris, http://www.oecd.org/tax/transparency/about-the-global-forum/publications/1998-consolidated-application-note.pdf. [4]

OECD (1998), *Harmful Tax Competition: An Emerging Global Issue*, OECD Publishing, Paris, https://dx.doi.org/10.1787/9789264162945-en. [1]

Annex B. Monitoring data on grandfathered non-IP regimes

1. Introduction

1.   The Forum on Harmful Tax Practices (FHTP) undertakes the review of preferential regimes in respect of all Inclusive Framework members. In addition to the review of the regimes, the FHTP conducts yearly monitoring with respect to certain type of regimes. This covers the following areas:

- IP regimes (with respect to the granting of benefits to the third category of IP assets and the use of the rebuttable presumption);

- Potentially harmful but not actually harmful regimes;

- Disadvantaged areas regimes; and

- Substantial activities with respect to non-IP regimes reviewed in 2017 and thereafter.

2.   Guidance on the closing off of regimes and grandfathering for non-IP regimes reviewed in 2017 and thereafter is published in Annex B of the 2017 Progress Report (OECD, 2017[3]). It mandates certain monitoring with respect to these type of regimes. This Annex B sets out the data points and process for carrying out this monitoring.

2. Approach to monitoring grandfathered non-IP regimes

3.   The scope of this monitoring exercise applies to a non-IP regime reviewed in 2017 and thereafter, which presents harmful features, and the jurisdiction has abolished or amended the regime, and where the harmful features of the previous form of the regime are grandfathered. It does not apply to regimes which are under review, are still in the process of being amended or eliminated, are found to be not harmful, are found to be out of scope, are found to be potentially harmful but not actually harmful, or where there is no grandfathering provided.

4.   The purpose of the monitoring of grandfathering for non-IP regimes is for the FHTP to have increased and continuing visibility on how jurisdictions are implementing the grandfathering provisions in practice. This monitoring mechanism ensures that jurisdictions are enforcing and implementing their grandfathering provisions in an effective way. The number of taxpayers in the grandfathered regime should either stay stable or decrease, since new taxpayers are not permitted into the grandfathered regime. If this is not the case, further information from the jurisdiction is required to identify the cause of the increase and to identify any remedial steps that should be taken to address the issue. This is also the case where the amount of income significantly increases, as new activities and assets are also not allowed in the grandfathered regime.

5.   To ensure that grandfathering is applied appropriately, the FHTP agreed to monitor the data on a yearly basis. The monitoring process commences from the time at

which the grandfathering period commences. For all regimes reviewed in 2017, the legislative process for amending or abolishing the regimes should be completed by 31 December 2018 at the latest, and it is only after this period that the grandfathering period would commence. The monitoring would cease after the data with respect to the end of the grandfathering period is reported. For the regimes reviewed in 2017, grandfathering will generally cease by June 2021 at the latest. Where the FHTP granted an exceptional extension of the grandfathering period as foreseen by paragraph 18 of the 2017 Progress Report (OECD, 2017[3]), no monitoring would be required as in those cases, additional spontaneous exchange of information requirements apply.

6.   There are two aspects to the monitoring: the data that should be collected, and the mode for making that data available to the FHTP.

3. Identifying the data that should be collected

7.   The information to be collected should include:

- A description of the mechanism to ensure new entrants (both new taxpayers and new assets/activities) entering the regime after the cut-off date (i.e. date of the FHTP's decision) are not benefiting from grandfathering;

- A description of the mechanism to ensure that benefits are not granted to those entitled to benefit from grandfathering after the end of the grandfathering period;

- The number of taxpayers benefitting from the regime in the close-off year (i.e. the year the regime is amended/abolished) and subsequent years where grandfathering is allowed;

- The amount of gross income benefitting from the grandfathering in the close-off year and subsequent years where grandfathering is allowed;

- The number of new taxpayers entering the regime in the period from the cut-off date (i.e. date of the publication of the decision by the Inclusive Framework) to the close-off date (i.e. by no later than 12 months from the cut-off date or where necessary because of the legislative process, by 31 December of the calendar year following the cut-off date); and

- Where a regime grants benefits to specific assets or activities, the total number of new assets and new activities entering the regime in the period from the cut-off date (i.e. date of the publication of the decision by the Inclusive Framework) to the close-off date (i.e. by no later than 12 months from the cut-off date or where necessary because of the legislative process, by 31 December of the calendar year following the cut-off date).

8.   These data points are designed to balance the administrative burden for the jurisdictions included in the monitoring process, and at the same time to ensure that the FHTP is able to identify any risks and to prompt further enquiry where necessary.

9.   Information with respect to all years for which grandfathering is available should be provided. In order for the FHTP to be able to make a comparison with the period before the regime was closed-off, economic data from the fiscal year before the grandfathering period started should be provided as well.

10.   In order for the FHTP to confirm that no benefits are provided after the grandfathering period, jurisdictions should also provide data with respect to the fiscal period after the latest grandfathering date (grandfathering end date).

11.   There are various ways that the data could be collected. For example, jurisdictions could collect the data via the taxpayer's tax returns, or they can introduce a specific annual reporting obligation for the taxpayer to the tax administration. If a ruling with respect to the preferential regime has been given to the taxpayer, information could be collected this way.

4. Mode for making the data available to the FHTP

12.   Annex B of the 2017 Progress Report (OECD, 2017[3]) states that the data on grandfathered non-IP regimes should be provided on an annual basis.

13.   The format for providing this data would be by way of a short questionnaire covering the above data points in paragraph 7. This would generally be completed in advance of the first FHTP meeting of each year by the relevant jurisdictions, starting from 2019. The compilation of questionnaires would generally be distributed for discussion at the first FHTP meeting of each year.

14.   If some of the statistical information is not yet available at the beginning of each year, for example because the tax return is filed later within the year, the jurisdiction would be asked to provide as much of the information as possible, and update the FHTP with the additional information as soon as it becomes available.

5. Possible outcomes of monitoring process

15.   The consideration of the monitoring data should be undertaken on a case by case basis, taking into account the relevant facts and circumstances. At the FHTP meeting where the monitoring data is presented, the FHTP would have the opportunity to ask questions relating to the grandfathered non-IP regime.

16.   If the jurisdiction's explanation of the mechanism is found to be sufficient by the FHTP and the monitoring data indicates that the numbers are relatively stable or decreasing, it would be expected that no discussion is required.

17.   If the monitoring data indicates a significant increase in the use of the regime and/or the FHTP does not find the jurisdiction's mechanisms and additional explanation to be sufficient, the FHTP should consider the types of additional data and information that is needed from the jurisdiction providing the grandfathering. Additional data and/or information should be provided in advance of the subsequent FHTP meeting. If there is no appropriate justification for the increase, the FHTP should give the jurisdiction a recommendation to address the issue and to ensure no tax benefits are granted inappropriately (or to reverse the granting of such tax benefits), as appropriate on a case-by-case basis. If the jurisdiction does not take steps to respond to the recommendation by the subsequent FHTP meeting, the FHTP could revisit the conclusion on the regime with respect to the grandfathering period. Any decision on the regime would be made on the basis of consensus minus one. In the event the jurisdiction does not provide the relevant information to the FHTP necessary to give the FHTP sufficient comfort on the implementation of the grandfathering provisions in practice, the jurisdiction would need to explain this and the FHTP may need then consider appropriate next steps.

References

OECD (2017), *Harmful Tax Practices - 2017 Progress Report on Preferential Regimes: Inclusive Framework on BEPS: Action 5*, OECD/G20 Base Erosion and Profit Shifting Project, OECD Publishing, Paris, https://dx.doi.org/10.1787/9789264283954-en. [3]

OECD (2015), *Countering Harmful Tax Practices More Effectively, Taking into Account Transparency and Substance, Action 5 - 2015 Final Report*, OECD/G20 Base Erosion and Profit Shifting Project, OECD Publishing, Paris, https://dx.doi.org/10.1787/9789264241190-en. [2]

OECD (2004), *Consolidated Application Note - Guidance in applying the 1998 report to preferential tax regimes*, OECD, Paris, http://www.oecd.org/tax/transparency/about-the-global-forum/publications/1998-consolidated-application-note.pdf. [4]

OECD (1998), *Harmful Tax Competition: An Emerging Global Issue*, OECD Publishing, Paris, https://dx.doi.org/10.1787/9789264162945-en. [1]

Annex C. Key reference documents

This Annex provides a list of key reference documents relevant to the work of the FHTP:

OECD (2018), Harmful Tax Practices – 2017 Peer Review Reports on the Exchange of Information on Tax Rulings: Inclusive Framework on BEPS: Action 5, OECD/G20 Base Erosion and Profit Shifting Project, OECD Publishing, Paris, https://doi.org/10.1787/9789264309586-en.

OECD (2017), Harmful Tax Practices - Peer Review Reports on the Exchange of Information on Tax Rulings: Inclusive Framework on BEPS: Action 5, OECD/G20 Base Erosion and Profit Shifting Project, OECD Publishing, Paris, https://doi.org/10.1787/9789264285675-en.

OECD (2017), Harmful Tax Practices - 2017 Progress Report on Preferential Regimes: Inclusive Framework on BEPS: Action 5, OECD/G20 Base Erosion and Profit Shifting Project, OECD Publishing, Paris. http://dx.doi.org/10.1787/9789264283954-en.

OECD (2017), BEPS Action 5 on Harmful Tax Practices – Terms of Reference and Methodology for the Conduct of the Peer Reviews of the Action 5 Transparency Framework, OECD/G20 Base Erosion and Profit Shifting Project, OECD, Paris. www.oecd.org/tax/beps/beps-action-5-harmful-tax-practices-peer-review-transparency-framework.pdf.

OECD (2015), *Countering Harmful Tax Practices More Effectively, Taking into Account Transparency and Substance, Action 5 - 2015 Final Report*, OECD/G20 Base Erosion and Profit Shifting Project, OECD Publishing, Paris, https://doi.org/10.1787/9789264241190-en.

OECD (2006) *The OECD's project on Harmful Tax Practices: 2006 update on progress in member countries*, OECD, Paris. www.oecd.org/tax/harmful/37446434.pdf.

OECD (2004) *The OECD's project on Harmful Tax Practices: the 2004 progress report*, OECD, Paris. www.oecd.org/ctp/harmful/oecd-harmful-tax-practices-project-2004-progress-report.pdf.

OECD (2004) *Consolidated application note guidance in applying the 1998 report to preferential tax regimes*, OECD, Paris. www.oecd.org/tax/transparency/about-the-global-forum/publications/1998-consolidated-application-note.pdf.

OECD (2001) *The OECD's project on Harmful Tax Practices: the 2001 progress report*, OECD, Paris. www.oecd.org/tax/harmful/2664438.pdf.

OECD (2000) *Towards Global Tax Co-operation - Report to the 2000 ministerial council meeting and recommendations by the Committee on Fiscal Affairs - Progress in Identifying and Eliminating Harmful Tax Practices*, OECD, Paris. www.oecd.org/tax/transparency/about-the-global-forum/publications/towards-global-tax-cooperation-progress.pdf.

OECD (1998), *Harmful Tax Competition: An Emerging Global Issue*, OECD Publishing, Paris, https://doi.org/10.1787/9789264162945-en.

ORGANISATION FOR ECONOMIC CO-OPERATION AND DEVELOPMENT

The OECD is a unique forum where governments work together to address the economic, social and environmental challenges of globalisation. The OECD is also at the forefront of efforts to understand and to help governments respond to new developments and concerns, such as corporate governance, the information economy and the challenges of an ageing population. The Organisation provides a setting where governments can compare policy experiences, seek answers to common problems, identify good practice and work to co-ordinate domestic and international policies.

The OECD member countries are: Australia, Austria, Belgium, Canada, Chile, the Czech Republic, Denmark, Estonia, Finland, France, Germany, Greece, Hungary, Iceland, Ireland, Israel, Italy, Japan, Korea, Latvia, Lithuania, Luxembourg, Mexico, the Netherlands, New Zealand, Norway, Poland, Portugal, the Slovak Republic, Slovenia, Spain, Sweden, Switzerland, Turkey, the United Kingdom and the United States. The European Union takes part in the work of the OECD.

OECD Publishing disseminates widely the results of the Organisation's statistics gathering and research on economic, social and environmental issues, as well as the conventions, guidelines and standards agreed by its members.

OECD PUBLISHING, 2, rue André-Pascal, 75775 PARIS CEDEX 16

(23 2018 58 1 P) ISBN 978-92-64-31147-3 – 2019

Printed by Libri Plureos GmbH in Hamburg, Germany